A REVIVALNOW! PUBLICATION

THE
BOOK *of* PRAYERS

adapted from the NIV Bible

Other Books by Wesley Campbell

Welcoming A Visitation Of The Holy Spirit

New Books currently Underway

The Radical Army
(with Stephen Court)

Praying The Bible: The Pathway to Spirituality

PRAYING THE BIBLE SERIES

THE
BOOK *of* PRAYERS

WESLEY & STACEY CAMPBELL

Foreword by Mike Bickle

REVIVALNOW! RESOURCES INC. KELOWNA B.C. CANADA

Published by RevivalNOW! Resources Inc. Kelowna, BC. Canada. Art Direction and design by Jeremy Crowle at Redant Digital Creativity. Cover Photography by Jeremy Crowle. Printed in Canada. Unless otherwise stated, all Scripture quotations taken from the HOLY BIBLE: NEW INTERNATIONAL VERSION ®. NIV ®.Copyright © 1973, 1978, 1984 by International Bible Society. Used by permission of Zondervan. The "NIV" and "New International Version" trademarks are registered in the United States Patent and Trademark Office by International Bible Society. Other versions used are: NKJV – Scripture taken from the New King James Version. Copyright © 1979, 1980, 1982 by Thomas Nelson Inc. All rights reserved

To Mike Bickle

---

who first taught me to pray the Bible,
and is now inspiring the world to pray
in International Houses Of Prayer (IHOPs) everywhere.

SECTION TWO - THE PSALMS

SECTION THREE - THE PRAYERS OF WISDOM

SECTION FOUR - THE SONG OF SONGS

SECTION FIVE - PRAYERS OF THE PROPHETS

SECTION SIX - THE PRAYERS OF JESUS

SECTION SEVEN - APOSTOLIC PRAYERS

SECTION EIGHT - HYMNS OF THE REVELATION

PREFACE

Prayer books are not new. As long ago as the time of Christ, the Jews had a body of prayers that was passed on through oral tradition. After the destruction of Jerusalem and the Temple and the final dispersion of the Jews in 70 AD, they were in danger of losing their prayer tradition. As a result, the Jews officially developed their own book of prayers. At the same time, the church was developing a tradition of prayer books with it's own distinct prayer culture. Centuries later, the wild Celtic church developed a 'pocket book' version of Psalms that doubled as a prayer book (c. 550 AD). Subsequently, small prayer books flourished everywhere. In the days of the Reformation and beyond, the Protestant church developed their own "Common Book of Prayers." Since then, virtually every branch of the Church has used prayer books.

Obviously, there is a pragmatic reason for all of the prayer books over the last two thousand years, and that reason is - they work! People don't do things that don't work. And because most people don't pray as well as they want to, they look for help. The experts, the ones who really do it, realize that to pray well they need not only words, but words that have substance in their content. Without the words – the prayers – most people cannot maintain momentum in intercession, and soon fall silent. When they grow silent, their minds wander, and by the time they realize it, they find themselves a million miles away from effective prayer. So, to correct this, the Church has always used prayer books.

Praying the Bible: The Book of Prayers attempts to give a new face to an old concept. The old concept is a prayer book. The new face is that the prayers have been laid out in eight distinct prayer genres. Short introductions have been prepared for each prayer style to assist children and novices, as well as seasoned intercessors, on how to pray the different styles. Altogether there are eighty-eight prayers directly from the Bible, arranged into eight major categories.

In *The Book of Prayers*, we have attempted to paraphrase the texts as little as possible. In the past, prayer books have often paraphrased the Bible beyond recognition, or strung together small sections of Scripture according to topic, so that there is not one complete text for the person praying to follow. Other prayer books contain the prayers of famous saints through the ages. It's not that we disdain these excellent efforts, but the difference here is that we have extracted concrete biblical prayers and presented the scriptural texts together in their entirety. A title has been assigned to each prayer, certain words have been either italicized or emboldened, and care has been taken in the placement and spacing of the verses, so that the layout naturally directs the one praying. The only exception to this pattern is in the section entitled 'The Prayers of Wisdom'. Here, the didactic nature of the literature has required verses to be gathered together and laid out in topical fashion with a minimal amount of paraphrasing in order to connect the thoughts, or shape the text into a 'prayable' prayer.

The prayers themselves are taken almost exclusively from the NIV translation of the Bible. There are a minimum of exceptions to this, one being the 'Prayer of Jabez,' which has utilized the NKJV, due to the popularity of the prayer in the book of the same title. As mentioned earlier, paraphrasing has been kept to a bare minimum, but there are cases where a phrase or a word has been altered or added, so that the prayer is easier to pray or more relevant to the modern reader. In some cases a name is deleted (as in 1 Chr. 17), or a space for your own name is provided (as in Dan.10). Occasionally, we have changed distinctly OT concepts to a NT equivalent. Examples of this would be 'temple' changed to 'kingdom' (1 Chr. 29); and 'sacrifices of bulls' and 'burnt offerings' changed to 'true worship' (Ps. 51). For " The Lord's Prayer," due to its sheer notoriety, we have used an adaptation of various translations, in order to form a composite of many versions, instead of using just one. Of course, any concerned intercessor can write their own notes and alterations into *The Book of Prayers* themselves, but it is hoped that the slight changes to the text are more helpful than bothersome. Wherever a prayer has been altered from the NIV, we have noted it with an asterisk (*), both in the table of contents, and after the prayer itself.

Allowances must also be made for the fact that some of these prayers are over three thousand years old. The accepted norm of writing in ancient times was to speak from a patriarchal, or male, perspective. We have left the text as it was written, but this is not meant to offend or belittle the female users. We judged that the transliterating of gender would have proved oner-ous to the intercessors themselves. In the case of 'The Prayers of Wisdom,' one must be sensitive to the style of writing, par-ticularly in the male/female designations (i.e. "adulteress" and "wisdom" which are female; "fool" and "king" which are male). It is assumed that both men and women will naturally allow for gender application, regardless whether it is a woman praying the 'The Prayers of Wisdom,' or men assuming the feminine bridal role in the Song of Songs. Readers must make the gender transla-tion and not let it be an obstacle.

It must also be noted that we have written and produced the book together. Therefore in the few times when the word 'I' is used, or an illustration is given from the perspective of one and not the other, this should be set in the context of the whole. That is, the whole was worked on by both of us, even though a few of the experiences are recorded as being singular.

The goal of *The Book of Prayers* was bring the main Bible prayers all together in a single volume, which would be small and functional. The print is bold and large enough for the user to be able to walk and pray easily. The teaching sections render the book self-explanatory for even the newest disciple. Parents who have wanted their children to memorize Scripture, will now be able to hand them *The Book of Prayers* and say: "... don't just memorize it ... pray it!" We hope that *The Book of Prayers* can become a working prayer book for intercessors and prayer rooms everywhere.

Bless you,
Wesley and Stacey Campbell

prayerispeace

prayerispeace

prayer

FOREWORD

By Mike Bickle

In 1979 the Lord called me to be an intercessor. Up until that time, I could count on one hand the hours I had spent in intercession. The entire concept was a mystery to me. What was intercession? How was I to do it? What good was it? For some time, I fumbled around trying to figure out how to obey God in this new thing that He was calling me to do.

Finally I realized that if I were going to pray at all, it would happen in real time and space. With that insight, I promptly scheduled fifteen prayer meetings every single week, all with different groups of people so that I would actually show up! Though we were faithful, I soon felt that this was not really getting us anywhere. The meetings were flat and aimless, and we weren't all that joyful about being there. There had to be a better way.

Then I thought, "Why not copy out the prayers of Paul, and pray those?" Excited with my new idea, I gathered up a few pages of white lined paper and scribbled out (in my own hand writing) a few of the Apostolic Prayers. The next day when the group showed up, I had photocopies of the various apostolic prayers of the NT for everyone. I was anxious to try out my new method. I held up one of 'Paul's' prayers and haltingly read it out loud to God. Everyone just looked at me. Then I said to the others, "Now it's your turn. Take one and pray it!" Somehow we made it through the first week . . . and the next . . . and then the next. Thus began the daily regiment of praying Bible prayers. We eventually grew into doing this three times a day for about seven years.

From those humble beginnings twenty years ago, God has now brought forth a movement with this new emphasis of praying the Bible, which is a key value in our 24-hour House of Prayer in Kansas City. At the "International House Of Prayer of Kansas City" (IHOP-KC), we offer up to Jesus worship and intercession 24 hours a day, 365 days a year. Trained and committed prayer missionaries fill 84 two-hour blocks of prayer each week, complete with prayer leaders, worship teams, sound crews, and the rank and file intercessors. The main staple of every 24-hour house of prayer is praying the Bible.

I've said all this to say, "That's why I rejoice to see Wesley and Stacey's new resource, *The Book of Prayers*." When I first met Wesley in 1989, he said he came to our annual conference because he struggled with prayer. As he learned to pray, the Lord put it on his heart to help others learn as well. This book is a result of that desire. Since those early days, Wesley and Stacey have also pioneered a whole expression of recordings with the "Praying The Bible" CDs. They have learned that when you give people the prayers, you give them the words which unlock their hearts. When Jesus' disciples asked Him to teach them to pray, He gave them a prayer, which has unlocked the hearts of multitudes.

As an advocate of regularly praying the Bible for the past twenty years, it's encouraging to see this old concept served up in a modern format. By arranging the prayers into eight distinct genres, every user will have instant access to whichever style he wants. The teaching behind the concept of "praying the Bible out loud to God every day," and the brief introductions at the beginning of each section, help even the newest Christians to understand how to make these prayers work for them. Prayer titles and page numbers make it possible for whole groups to pray in an organized corporate fashion – that is, everyone can lock into the same passage with the same translation for an extended period of time.

Praying the Bible: The Book of Prayers is the prayer manual you have been waiting for. Every church and every prayer room should have a generous supply. Pastors everywhere can mobilize their whole congregation to pray Bible prayers through this easy-to-use tool. I encourage parents to gather their families together and pray these prayers with their children. I guarantee that if you pray *The Book of Prayers*, first your communion with God will change, then your life will change . . . and in the course of time, the whole world will change.

Mike Bickle
Founder, International House of Prayer of Kansas City
www.fotb.com

prayerispeace

prayerispeace

INTRODUCTION

THE BOOK OF PRAYERS

Those who have determined in their hearts to develop a relationship with God will ultimately be driven to the place of prayer. There is no way around it. In the Bible, the greatest men and women of the Spirit were men and women of prayer. Scripture says, "Elijah was a man just like us, and *he prayed earnestly* that it would not rain on the land for three and a half years. *Again he prayed* and the heavens gave rain, and the earth produced its crops" (James 5:17). Think about that. Elijah was a man just like you! When he prayed, it stopped raining for three and a half years, a dead boy was raised, and fire came down from heaven. He communicated with God in a manner that most Christians know nothing about. Noah and Abraham also bowed down to God. Isaac said, "truly God is in this place," so he set up an altar where he called upon God. Jacob wrestled with the angel of the Lord throughout the night. Moses spent days and nights in prayer. The record says that he went daily to the tent of the Lord, and Joshua went with him – and stayed longer (Ex. 33:7-11)! Samuel prayed. David wanted to gaze on God's beauty every day of his life (Ps. 27:4). He "cried to the Lord morning, noon, and night" (Ps. 55:17), and meditated on God "through the night watches" (Ps. 63:6). Daniel was in the practice of praying three times every day (Dan. 6:10). It is a serious error to gloss over the prayer lives of the patriarchs of our faith, thinking we can imitate their works apart from imitating their prayer lives.

Our most striking prayer example, however, is Jesus himself. How incredible that the perfect God-man seems to pray more than anyone else. He is always praying, and he instructs us to pray always (Lk. 18:1). In one sense, this is confusing. Why did Jesus, the God-man, have to pray so much? If anybody should be exempt from prayer, it would be him. Yet he lived his life as though it really mattered that he prayed! In fact, nearly every chapter in the gospel of Luke shows Jesus praying. Luke records that from the beginning of his public ministry, Jesus prayed. "When all the people were being baptized, Jesus was baptized too, and *as He was praying* heaven was opened" (Luke 3:21). This one statement encapsulates the ministry of Jesus – "*as He was praying, heaven was opened.*" Immediately following this prayer, Jesus is driven by the Spirit into the wilderness, where again he enters into a major prayer time, complete with fasting, for forty days (Mk 1:12-13, Lk. 4:1-2).

As news about Jesus spread, crowds came to hear him and be healed of their sicknesses. What was Jesus' response to this? He "often withdrew to lonely places and prayed" (Lk.5:16). The optimum word here is *'often'*! Prayer, for Jesus, was not a one off thing. He would even spend whole nights in prayer. Before the critical decision of calling his disciples, ". . . Jesus went out to a mountainside to pray, and *spent the night praying* to God" (Lk.6:12). His prayer life was so dynamic that he experienced dramatic manifestations. While he prayed, his face and clothes changed their appearance (Luke 9:28-29), and sweat fell to the ground like great drops of blood (Luke 22:44). He groaned, cried loudly, and wept during his times of intercession (Hebrews 5:7). He got up early and stayed up late – just to pray (Mark 1:35-38). Further, Jesus maintained that Temple life was all about prayer. "It is written," he said to them, "My house will be called a *house of prayer*, but you have made it a 'den of robbers'" (Luke 19:46). He prayed for his disciples, and he prayed for us (John 17:9, 20). Jesus was always praying.

Why did he do this? Did Jesus know something we don't? Did he understand that spiritual authority – even his own – came through prayer, because prayer is *the* mechanism that produces relationship with the Father? Did Jesus really believe that he could do nothing by himself? Did he know that if he did not pray, there would be no mighty works? Perhaps he understood that he could receive more words, more power, and more authority to do the Father's will if he prayed? He also seemed to instinctively know when it was time to withdraw and pray (Lk. 5:42). Because of this, 'the work' was never allowed to distract him from his source of power for 'the work'.

Those who were closest to Jesus recognized that there was something different about the way he prayed, so they asked him to teach them how to pray. "Master," they said, "teach us to pray as John taught his disciples to pray" (Luke 11:1). Gladly, Jesus responded. In essence, he said, "You do it like this: You 'ought always to pray and not stop' (Luke 18:1). You 'watch and pray that you don't fall into temptation' (Mt. 26:41). You 'go into your closet alone and pray in secret so that the Father who sees you in secret will would reward you openly'" (Matt 6:6).

Frankly, every Christian must come to terms with the fact that Jesus, as well as Moses, Daniel, David, Elijah, John the Baptist, and the rest, actually practiced continual prayer and because of this they had more power and authority than anyone else. How can we see the direct correlation between their consistent prayer lives and the great power and authority they walked in, and not be inspired to imitate their example?

After twenty years of full time Christian work, we are convinced that the reason most people do not pray is not because they are fundamentally disobedient or unspiritual – it's just that they don't know how. For my part, I spent the better part of a decade trying to teach myself how to pray and get others praying as well. This prayer book is the distillation of twelve years of work, trying to learn how to pray.

My first discovery was that people in every place and at every time have 'prayed the Bible'. It was shocking to find that for thousands of years, men and women of God have used the model of praying the Bible – out loud – to God – everyday! Virtually every denomination of the Church has done this. From the starting point of praying the Bible out loud, many have moved into advanced stages of silent or *infused* prayer. Yet everyone learns to walk before they run. To reach the mountaintop of silent prayer, one must first climb the various plateaus of vocal prayer. In time, we will naturally move into places of silence. However, the starting place for Christians has always been the same – praying the Bible out loud. It might even be said that modern day evangelical/charismatic Christianity may be the first sector of the Church in over three thousand years to 'not do prayer right!'

When we look deeper into the prayer life of Jesus, we discover some interesting patterns. We know that Jesus was Jewish and, as a Jew, he was brought up "according to the custom"

(Lk. 2:22; 2:42; 4:16). What most modern readers don't know is that the Jewish custom of prayer was very defined in Jesus' day. It originated in the first books of the Old Testament and was based on a very literal understanding of the Scriptures. The first major commandment on prayer is found in the greatest of all Jewish commandments, the *Shema*.

> *Hear, O Israel: The LORD our God, the LORD is one. Love the LORD your God with all your heart and with all your soul and with all your strength. These commandments that I give you today are to be upon your hearts. Impress them on your children. Talk about them when you sit at home and when you walk along the road, when you lie down and when you get up. Tie them as symbols on your hands and bind them on your foreheads. Write them on the doorframes of your houses and on your gates. . ." (Deut. 6:4-9)*

According to the Babylonian Talmud, Jewish boys were taught this passage as soon as they could speak (*Sukkah 42a*). It further specifies that the "the *father* must teach him." It is safe to assume, therefore, that Joseph taught his son, Jesus, how to pray this passage. In fact, the *Shema* is central to the whole of Jewish life. In his classic work, *To Be A Jew*, Rabbi Donin writes:

> *. . . to engage in prayer is the most obvious and the most universal reflection of man's relationship with God. Prayer in its highest form and at its most sincere levels is called a 'service of the heart,' and constitutes one of the many ways by which love of God is expressed.[1]*

As you can see, for every Jew, the *Shema* was a call to prayer. And prayer, according to the Rabbis, was a proof of one's love for God. Simply put, the first of the Ten Commandments – "to worship the Lord your God" (Ex. 20; Deut. 5), the *Shema* – "to love the Lord your God" (Deut. 6:5), and the oft repeated commandment "to serve the Lord your God" (Deut. 10:12; 11:13, etc.), are all fulfilled by prayer. Prayer becomes at once the means and proof of love. This tradition of prayer among Jews as a "service of the heart" was the tradition that Jesus was raised in.

Tradition would have also dictated that Jesus prayed *every day*. Throughout the Bible, we see that the people of God prayed "day and night," "continuously" and "without ceasing." Of course, the obvious question is whether God is really serious about having his people pray "day and night?" What does "day and night" really mean? Is it just a religious cliché? How Israel understood Deut. 6:4-13 and Josh. 1:8 is evidenced by how they lived it out. When Zachariah went into the holy of holies and "the time for the burning of incense came, all the assembled worshipers were praying outside" (Lk. 1:10). How early this practice started we cannot know, but when Moses would go into the tent of meeting to talk to God, all of the Israelites worshiped at the entrance of their own tents (Ex. 33:8-10). By the time of David, we know that morning and evening prayers were becoming the norm within Tabernacle/Temple worship. David said, "I call to God and the LORD saves me. *Evening, morning and noon*, I cry out in distress, and he hears my voice" (Ps 55:16-17). David's prescribed pattern in the Temple was to have morning and evening prayer.

Since David believed the sacrifices should be accompanied with morning and evening prayers, he called for "the Levites to help Aaron's descendants in the service of the temple of the LORD . . .They were also to stand *every morning* to thank and praise the LORD. They were to do the same *in the evening*" (1 Chr. 23:28, 30). Daniel carried this practice to the point of obsession as a captive in Babylon where, under threat of death, he refused to break his habit of praying three times daily. *"Three times a day he got down on his knees and prayed*, giving thanks to his God, just as he had done before" (Dan. 6:10). Historians tell us that sometime after the seventy years of captivity in Babylon (c. 450 B.C.), Ezra determined that Israel would never again provoke God to such wrath. So, he mandated daily prayers, accompanied with readings from the *Torah*. In time, it became custom for Jews to pray the eighteen "Benedictions," coupled with readings from the *Torah*, over three set 'hours' of prayer at the temple, synagogue, or home. This custom was firmly in place long before the birth of Jesus. Accordingly, Jesus along with every righteous Jew, would have observed this practice daily. It is interesting to think that Jesus, his father Joseph, and Joseph's father, all would have prayed this way; that Peter, James, and John grew up praying set prayers every day; and that Paul was steeped in the model of Jewish prayer.

The evidence from the New Testament is that 'night and day' prayer was practiced by the entire early church, as well as by the God-fearers who had attached themselves to Judaism. Luke records "Peter and John were going up to the temple at the ninth [hour], the hour of prayer" (Acts 3:1). Cornelius, a Gentile God-fearer is called a devout man who 'prayed continually'. The next verse explains what continual prayer means: "About the ninth hour of the day [the hour of prayer] he clearly saw in a vision an angel of God who came to him, and said to him, 'Cornelius!' . . . 'Your prayers and alms have ascended as a memorial before

God'" (Acts 10:2-4).

Hourly prayer is further implied when Peter goes up to his housetop to pray: "it was about the sixth hour" – the noon time of prayer" (Acts 9:9). The outpouring of Pentecost occurred at the ninth hour" – a time of prayer (Acts 2:15). It says of the early church born at Pentecost that, "those who believed were daily (and continually) in the temple courts as well as meeting from house to house" (Lk. 24:53; Acts 2:26). What did they do 'daily in the temple courts?' Jesus said they prayed. With fury he demanded: "My house (the *temple*) shall be called a *house of prayer* for all nations" (Mk. 11:17), and earlier described how "two men went up to the temple *to pray*" (Lk. 18:10). The early church was not celebrating or gossiping in the temple courts. They were praying 'daily and continually' – fulfilling the customary hours of prayer.

As you can see, both the Jews and the early church prayed a minimum of three set times of prayer. The first hour ranged from 6:00 AM to 9:00 AM, the second was at noon, and the third somewhere between 3:00 PM and 6:00 PM. Whether they felt like it or not, whether they knew how to do it or not, whether they felt inspired or not, as worshippers of God they were just called to show up. Jesus and the apostles did this and, like them, we are called to do it as well. Like them, we need to set a time, and make a place, to get face-to-face with God.

The other practice of Jesus was that he *prayed the Bible.* The Jews had a body of prayers that had been passed on through oral tradition. These prayers were all based on the Law of God, which God gave us from the beginning. Joshua was told specifically to ". . . meditate on the *Book of the Law* day and night." David put this into practice, and we got the Psalms (Ps. 1:2). The prophets did it, and we got the prophetic books. Ultimately, the expansion of the Law and the prophets make up what Jesus called "the Scriptures" (Lk. 24:27). These are the words that have been given to us to pray. Paul put it this way: "This is what we speak, not in words taught us by human wisdom, but in words taught by the Spirit, expressing *spiritual truths in spiritual words*" (1 Cor. 2:13). The whole Bible is God-breathed; it is the language of the Spirit – the language of prayer.

Throughout history, the Church has taught the faithful to pray by praying the Bible. No section of the Church has ever questioned this time-honored method. As far back as our Judaistic roots, on into the NT, the Desert Fathers, and throughout Church history, the saints and all believers were taught to "pray the Bible." Virtually every famous Christian through the ages has preached and practiced praying the Bible.

Thus, *Praying the Bible – The Book of Prayers* becomes the modern-day application of an ancient tradition. The categories of prayer are laid out in chronological order, just as they appear in the Bible. They are:

•*The Theophanies*
•*The Psalms*
•*The Prayers of Wisdom*
•*The Song of Songs*
•*The Prayers of the Prophets*
•*The Prayers of Jesus*
•*The Apostolic Prayers*
•*The Hymns of the Revelation*

Also, in order to facilitate effective prayer, a detailed description of how to pray each section is provided in the introductions. This prayer book continues the practice that even Jesus himself did – the praying of the Law back to God.

Lastly, when Jesus prayed the Bible, he did it out loud. Hebrews 5:7 says, "During the days of Jesus' life on earth, he offered up prayers and petitions with loud cries and tears . . . and he was heard because of his reverent submission." Does this mean that, we have to cry bitterly and pray loudly in order to be heard? The obvious answer is No! But the not so obvious implication is that a person cannot cry or pray loudly unless they are deeply immersed in what they are doing. Jesus was emotionally engaged when he prayed. He was wholly taken over by his prayer. He was sweating and weeping because he was into it.

Do you know another major reason why God wants you to pray the Bible out loud? Most people don't. The reason simply is, "So you know when you've stopped!" If you think about it for a moment, you will see the simple wisdom of this statement. Praying out loud solves the problem of the "wandering mind." The Desert Father, St. Cassian said, *"The man who prays only when on his knees, prays little. The man who kneels to pray and then lets his mind wander, prays not at all."* An antidote for the malady of the wandering mind is prescribed in the very word given by God when he commanded the Israelites to pray in Josh. 1:8. That word is *meditate.* Wrongly, most of us have interpreted the phrase 'to meditate' as something we do silently. Even worse, some understand it in the context of Eastern religions, where it involves the emptying of one's self to achieve *nirvana (*or nothingness). All of this is a gross misunderstanding of what the word "meditate" means. Strong's definition of the Hebrew word for "meditate – *hagah"* means: "to imagine, meditate, mourn, mutter, roar, speak, study, talk, utter." The International Standard Bible Encyclopaedia, interprets it as "to murmur, to have a deep tone, to sigh, moan," or *higgayon*, "the murmur or dull sound of the harp." This is biblical meditation.

In the Bible, equivalents of *hagah* are as follows: "the lion roars or growls (*hagah*) over his prey" (Isa. 31:4); "we moan (*hagah*) like doves" (Isa. 59:11); "mediums and spiritists whisper and mutter (*hagah*)" (Isa. 8:19). From these contexts we discern that *hagah,* (meditate) meant "to say over and over again, to speak, to mutter, to recite, to expel air out loud." There was to be physical involvement in this activity. And, in the case of Joshua, he was to *hagah* – to say over and over again – the Book of the Law *out loud* to God.

Obviously, when this command was given to ancient Israel, they didn't have many copies of the Law. Unlike today, the average Israelite family would not have had their own personalized scroll of the Book of the Law. So how they learned it (in order to meditate upon it) was by *oral recitation*. They would gather in groups to chant the Law. Later, the men would pass on what they learned to their families at home (Duet. 6:4 –13). That is why every letter of the Hebrew Scriptures is set to musical notations, or *tropes*, which make memorization possible and facilitate vocal meditation. Some of the Psalms and Proverbs are even structured in the style of musical acrostics (Ps. 119; Prov. 31). It was almost like an ancient form of Hebrew rap, if you will. In this manner, they passed the commandments on to their children and developed the power to 'do' the Law itself. They prayed the words out loud back to God until the Law took root in their hearts. To this very day, Jews pray out loud. We have all seen them at the Wailing Wall in prayer, bobbing and rocking as they mutter the Law. Their whole body is involved in meditation. It is not merely a mental exercise, or a passive contemplation. No, it is an engaging recitation of a specific text to the Lord. One could say that they used their mouths . . . to lasso their minds . . . to affect their spirits.

All of this may sound strange to non-traditional ears. However, if the truth were known, the modern Islamic practice of praying five times a day, by reciting scriptures out loud while facing Mecca (instead of Jerusalem), is closer to NT prayer than we think. In fact, the five pillars of Islam – their statement of faith, daily prayer (five times a day), almsgiving, fasting, and a pilgrimage to their holy site, were all copied from common and prevalent practices of the Church at that time (7th century A.D.). The sad thing is that the prayer practice Muslims copied from Christianity, and now practice out of legalism, Christians will not practice out of love. But, the fact remains – the pathway to spirituality is found in praying the Bible. That is why every family needs to be intent on "praying the Bible – out loud – to God – everyday!"

prayerispeace *prayer*

Theophan

THEOPHANIES

In the thirtieth year, while I was among
the exiles by the Kebar River, the heavens were
opened and I saw visions of God.

INTRODUCTION TO PRAYING THE THEOPHANIES

What are the *'theophanies'* and why begin *The Book of Prayers* with these selections of Scripture? These two questions must be answered at the outset as they greatly affect the way we pray. The Bible commands us to pray, to meditate, and to recite the law *to God*. Of course, people of every religion pray, and they all think they are praying *to God*. But who is right? Which God is the true God? Where is he? What is he like? What is he doing? These are questions that any worshipper will consider when they set aside time to talk *to God*.

Often, when speaking on the topic of prayer, I ask a congregation to stand up so that I can give them a test. The question I give them is this: "If you know the location of at least four of the many God sightings in the Bible, and you can generally recount what the prophet saw . . . then stay standing." At first people begin to look around, dumbfounded. Then slowly, with sheepish, sideways glances, almost everyone begins to sit down. Rarely is there even three percent of the audience left standing. Almost no one is in the regular practice of praying the *theophanies* – that is the 'God sightings.'

It's hard to overstate the seriousness of this spiritual omission. For instance, imagine if seven of the most holy, prophetically-inspired men and women of all of Christendom made a pilgrimage to a mountain, where they fasted and prayed for a week for a breakthrough with God. Imagine that God actually came down in a full-blown, visible display of his glory. Imagine that these seven were overwhelmed and laid low in the awesome presence of God. Then, as soon as they were able, they came down and declared that they had seen God with their eyes and that they would be gathering at a specific time and place to tell about it. Who wouldn't want to be there? Who wouldn't want to read a detailed account?

Yet we have the greatest holy men of history – men like Moses (Ex. 24 & 34), Isaiah (Isa. 6), Daniel (Dan. 7 & 10), Ezekiel (Ez. 1 & 10), Peter (Matt. 17), and John (Rev. 1, 4, 19, 21) – all of whom say they saw God (or the glorified Christ) with their eyes and wrote down what they saw. How absurd is it, then, for believers who have given their whole lives to love and serve God, who say they believe in the inspiration and inerrancy of these accounts, not even to know where they are found, much less be able to recite them in their minds and spirits?

The word *theophanies* comes from two Greek words: *theos,* meaning 'God,' and *phaino,* meaning 'to appear or show'; hence, the 'God appearances'. It is the details of these 'God sightings' that let us in on what God looks like and, to some extent, on what God is doing. They describe, at different times, where he lives, who is around him, the color of his hair and eyes, what he is wearing, the many sounds of his voice, etc . . . As such, they should become our starting point in prayer because, unless we are praying *to God* as he has revealed himself to be, we are not really praying in the Christian sense of the word. We must know the One to whom we are talking, so that we are not just worrying with our eyes closed. God is a Person, and it is to this Person that all of our prayers must be directed. Therefore, when you pray the *theophanies,* you will 'see' just who it is that you are talking to. You will become familiar with the sights and sounds of heaven. You will have confidence that your prayers are not only being heard, but that you are addressing the one Person who has all power in heaven and on earth to answer them. And, if you pray them long enough, your relationship with God will change. As you address him as he is, revelation will pour out of each one of his attributes. Intimacy and communion will flow between you and God as the Holy Spirit unveils him and leads us into "all truth" about who he really is.

When we pray the *theophanies* we begin to touch his power, to hear that loud voice like many waters, to tremble in the presence of the thunders and lightening bolts. Any person who does not at some time pray the *theophanies* will likely limit God. To them, God may become smaller than he really is, because the person will be praying *to God* as they understand him to be, not as he has revealed himself to be. After all, God is who he says he is – not who we think he is! So it is essential to begin all prayer by praying to the Person of God, and praying the *theophanies* will keep us from praying to an extension of our own darkened minds.

Also, praying the *theophanies* will also reveal that there is another entire world going on besides this base plain on which we live. *Yahweh* has a heavenly council that convenes to discuss affairs on earth (Job 1; 1 Kings 22). The *theophanies* illustrate that there are multiple ranks of angels, with magnificent powers, surrounding God in heaven. All of these awesome beings have the capacity for independent thought and action. They offer their council and volunteer for service. They exist in a host of different levels with different functions, beauties and strengths. You will learn how this other world intersects with our world (Dan. 10 etc.) – how it impacts it, moves it, changes it, and communicates with it. Soon, like Elisha's servant, you will realize that "greater are they that are for us than those that are against us." Your faith will take on prophetic proportions. All of this will come alive in your spirit by repeatedly praying the *theophanies*.

That a fuller understanding of God will be gained by praying the *theophanies,* is evidenced by examining the visions of Daniel. In Daniel 7, a comprehensive and advanced vision of God emerges. Here God appears as an old man, revealing himself as the "Ancient of Days." Whether God is old or whether this was the visage he chose in order to identify with Daniel in his old age, we can only surmise. Interestingly, another figure, *'one like a son of man'* is also introduced at this point for the first time in Scripture. Daniel does not ascribe to him the traditional 'Angel of the Lord' title, in fact, this mysterious second personality in Daniel seems to be described in terms that were previously reserved for God himself. Initially, the 'one like a son of man' comes in the clouds (7:13). In praying the *theophonies*, seasoned intercessors will know that if the clouds do not indicate divinity in this case, then this would be the only exception in about seventy-five passages featuring 'cloud/s' in the Old Testament where they do accompany or symbolize divinity.[1] Of course, when Daniel wrote this, he would have no concept of the 'Trinity,' or that God had a 'Son,' or that the Son was pre-existent before he was incarnated as a human. And what is more, as a strict monotheist, all of this flew in the face of everything he knew about "the LORD your God is One." In the end all he could say was, "I Daniel did not understand" (12:8), but he did know what he saw!

It is only after the birth of Christ, that all the pieces of revelation come together.

Even though Daniel does not understand all of what he sees and hears, the NT provides a fuller understanding of the mysterious 'angel of the Lord' and of the 'one like a son of man'. In the trial of Jesus,

> . . . the high priest asked him, 'Are you the Christ, the Son of the Blessed One? Are you then the Son of God?' 'I am,' said Jesus. 'And you will see the Son of Man sitting at the right hand of the Mighty One and coming on the clouds of heaven.' At this saying, 'the high priest tore his clothes' and asked, 'Why do we need any more witnesses? You have heard the blasphemy'(Mark 14:61-64, Luke 22:70).

Jesus himself referred to the *theophany* to describe who he was and in so doing, he was making a declaration of his divinity, ultimately causing himself to be condemned as worthy of death.

Further, the most detailed vision of the Christ prior to the NT – "the glorious man in linen," is found in Daniel 10. This *theophany* provides more details on the Christ than either Moses, Isaiah or Ezekiel. He is seen as superior to Michael (10:13), and as 'sent' by (implied) a greater (10:11). A careful study will show that virtually every descriptive word of the "Heavenly Man" correlates exactly with the descriptive words used by John in Rev. 1:13-16. It is almost unimaginable that this "glorious man" is not the pre-incarnate Christ that John will see hundreds of years later on the Island of Patmos. That being the case, the insights gained from what he says (Dan 10 – 12), and the awareness of the battles he wages, are gems not found anywhere else in Scripture. Who among us would not want to know everything "the Son of Man" was up to hundreds of years before he appeared as a baby on earth? Praying the *theophanies* will tell you.

From just this one example, it is evident how praying the *theophanies* will lead you to a much fuller understanding of the Godhead. The nuances are more than could fill a book. Practically, the way to pray the *theophanies* is to recite them *out loud to God* as they are written until you are absolutely familiar with each encounter. Then with a thorough understanding of each of the heavenly visions, begin to insert your own name in place of Daniel's, Ezekiel's, etc.... You should imagine and believe that similar things are happening in the spirit as you pray today, just as they were happening when the prophets prayed way back when. You may even change the name of the principality in the text (see Dan. 10) to the names of those principalities over your own country or over those for whom you are interceding. Like Daniel, we may not understand everything we see and pray, because the finite will never completely understand the Infinite. However, we will be able to go much deeper into God than we could have gone without meditating on these visions of God.

All of this brings us back to the fact that praying the *theophanies* will reveal God as he really is. And if men and women, and especially children are ever going to pray effectively, they must first start by being able to *see* him. We must pray the *theophonies* until heaven becomes as familiar to us as our own homes. Our children must be able to close their eyes and see God sitting on the throne, envision the sea of glass, and hear the living creatures in heaven, with all of the corresponding movement, color, and sound. Imagine if we were able to mentally walk through the surroundings of heaven and have them be as familiar as our earthly surroundings. My advice to everyone is always the same: "Both you and your children should begin to pray Revelation 4 at least one hundred times out loud to God – ten times a day for ten days straight. Then you will see God!" And, since prayer is talking *to God*, a great place to begin is with the *theophanies*, because they show us who God really is.

VISIONS OF GOD

In the thirtieth year,
in the fourth month on the fifth day,
while I was among the exiles by the Kebar River,
the heavens were opened and I saw visions of God.

There the hand of the LORD was upon me.

I looked,
and I saw a windstorm coming out of the north—
an immense cloud with flashing lightning
and surrounded by brilliant light.

The center of the fire looked like glowing metal,
and in the fire was what looked like *four living creatures*.
In appearance their *form* was that of a *man*,
but each of them had *four faces* and *four wings*.

Their *legs* were straight;
their *feet* were like those of a calf
and gleamed like burnished bronze.

Under their *wings* on their four sides
they had the *hands of a man*.
All four of them had faces and wings,
and their wings touched one another.
Each one went straight ahead;
they did not turn as they moved.

Their faces looked like this:
Each of the four had the face of a ***man***,
and on the right side each had the face of a ***lion***,
and on the left the face of an ***ox***;
each also had the face of an ***eagle***.
Such were their faces.

Their wings were spread out upward;
each had two wings,
one touching the wing of another creature on either side,
and two wings covering its body.

Each one went straight ahead.
Wherever the Spirit would go, they would go,
without turning as they went.

The appearance of the living creatures
was like burning coals of fire or like torches.
Fire moved back and forth among the creatures;
it was bright, and lightning flashed out of it.
The creatures sped back and forth like flashes of lightning.

As I looked at the living creatures,
I saw a wheel on the ground beside each creature
with its four faces.

This was the appearance and structure of the wheels:
They sparkled like chrysolite,
and all four looked alike.
Each appeared to be made like a wheel intersecting a wheel.

As they moved,
they would go in any one of the four directions
the creatures faced;
the wheels did not turn about as the creatures went.

Their rims were high and awesome,
and all four rims were **full of eyes** all around.

When the living creatures moved,
the wheels beside them moved;
and when the living creatures rose from the ground,
the wheels also rose.

Wherever the Spirit would go,
they would go,
and the wheels would rise along with them,
because the Spirit of the living creatures was in the wheels.

When the creatures moved, they also moved;
when the creatures stood still, they also stood still;
and when the creatures rose from the ground,
the wheels rose along with them,
because the Spirit of the living creatures was in the wheels.

Spread out above the heads of the living creatures was what
looked like an expanse, sparkling like ice, and awesome.

Under the expanse their wings were stretched out
one toward the other,
and each had two wings covering its body.

When the creatures moved,
I heard the sound of their wings,
like the roar of rushing waters,
like the voice of the Almighty,
like the tumult of an army.
When they stood still,
they lowered their wings.

Then there came a voice
from above the expanse over their heads
as they stood with lowered wings.
Above the expanse over their heads
was what looked like a throne of sapphire,
and high above on the throne was a figure like that of a man.

I saw that from what appeared to be his waist up
He looked like glowing metal, as if full of fire,
and that from there down He looked like fire;
and brilliant light surrounded Him.
Like the appearance of a rainbow in the clouds on a rainy day,
so was the radiance around Him.

This was the appearance . . .
of the likeness . . . of the glory of the LORD.

When I saw it, I fell face down,
and I heard the voice of One speaking.

Ezekiel 1:1-28

YAHWEH AND THE TEN COMMANDMENTS

On the morning of the third day
there was **thunder** and **lightning**,
with **a thick cloud** over the mountain,
and a very **loud trumpet** blast.
Everyone in the camp trembled.
Then Moses led the people out of the camp to meet with God,
and they stood at the foot of the mountain.

Mount Sinai was covered with **smoke**,
because the **LORD** descended on it in **fire**.
The **smoke billowed up** from it like smoke from a furnace,
the whole **mountain trembled** violently,
and the **sound** of the trumpet grew **louder and louder**.

Then Moses spoke and the **voice** of God answered him.
The **LORD** descended to the top of Mount Sinai
and called Moses to the top of the mountain.

The ***LORD*** replied,
Go down and bring Aaron up with you.
But the priests and the people must not force their way through
to come up to the ***LORD***, or He will break out against them.
So Moses went down to the people and told them.

And God spoke all these words:

I am the LORD your God,
who brought you out of Egypt, out of the land of slavery.

You shall have no other gods before Me.

You shall not make for yourself an idol
in the form of anything in heaven above or on the earth beneath
or in the waters below. You shall not bow down to them or
worship them; ***for I, the LORD your God, am a jealous God,***
punishing the children for the sin of the fathers to the third
and fourth generation of those who hate me, but showing love
to a thousand generations of those who love Me and keep My
commandments.

You shall not misuse the name of the LORD your God,
for the **LORD** will not hold anyone guiltless who misuses His
name.

Remember the Sabbath day by keeping it holy.
Six days you shall labor and do all your work, but the seventh
day is a Sabbath to the **LORD** your God. On it you shall not
do any work, neither you, nor your son or daughter, nor your
manservant or maidservant, nor your animals, nor the alien
within your gates. For in six days the **LORD** made the heavens
and the earth, the sea, and all that is in them, but He rested on
the seventh day. Therefore the **LORD** blessed the Sabbath day
and made it holy.

Honor your father and your mother,
so that you may live long in the land the **LORD** your God is
giving you.

You shall not murder.

You shall not commit adultery.

You shall not steal.

You shall not give false testimony against your neighbor.

You shall not covet your neighbor's house.
You shall not covet your neighbor's wife, or his manservant or
maidservant, his ox or donkey, or anything that belongs to your
neighbor.

When the people saw the **thunder** and **lightning**
and heard the **trumpet** and saw the **mountain** in **smoke**,
they trembled with fear.
They stayed at a distance and said to Moses,
"Speak to us yourself and we will listen.
But do not have God speak to us or we will die."

Moses said to the people,
*"Do not be afraid. God has come to test you,
so that the fear of God will be with you
to keep you from sinning."*

The people remained at a distance,
while Moses approached the thick darkness where God was.

Exodus 19:16-20; 24-25; 20:1- 21

SHOW ME YOUR GLORY

Then Moses said to Him,
***"If Your Presence does not go with us,
do not send us up from here.***
How will anyone know
that You are pleased with me
and with Your people
unless You go with us?
What else will distinguish me and Your people
from all the other people on the face of the earth?"

And the **LORD** said to Moses,
*"I will do the very thing you have asked,
because I am pleased with you
and I know you by name."*

Then Moses said,
"Now show me Your glory."

And the **LORD** said,
***"I will cause all my goodness
to pass in front of you,
and I will proclaim My name,
the LORD,***
*in your presence.
I will have mercy
on whom I will have mercy,
and I will have compassion
on whom I will have compassion.*

Then the **LORD** came down in the cloud
and stood there with him
and proclaimed His name,
the LORD.

And He passed in front of Moses, proclaiming,

"The LORD,
the LORD, the compassionate and gracious God,
slow to anger,
abounding in love and faithfulness,
maintaining love to thousands,
and forgiving wickedness,
rebellion and sin.

Yet he does not leave the guilty unpunished;
he punishes the children
and their children
for the sin of the fathers
to the third and fourth generation."

Moses bowed to the ground at once
and worshiped.

When Moses came down from Mount Sinai
with the two tablets of the Testimony in his hands,
he was not aware that his face was radiant
because he had spoken with the LORD.

Exodus 33:15 – 19, 34:5-8, 29

EYES AND WINGS

I looked,
and I saw the likeness of a throne of sapphire
above the expanse that was over the heads of the **cherubim**.

The **LORD** said to the man clothed in linen,
"Go in among the wheels beneath the *cherubim*.
Fill your hands with burning coals from among the *cherubim*
and scatter them over the city."
And as I watched, he went in.

Now the *cherubim* were standing on the south side of the
temple when the man went in,
and a cloud filled the inner court.

Then the glory of the LORD rose from above the cherubim
and moved to the threshold of the temple.
The cloud filled the temple,
and the court was full of the radiance of the glory of the
LORD.

The sound of the wings of the *cherubim* could be heard
as far away as the outer court,
like the voice of *God Almighty* when he speaks.

When the *LORD* commanded the man in linen,
"Take fire from among the **wheels**,
from among the *cherubim*,"
the man went in and stood beside a wheel.

Then one of the *cherubim* reached out his hand
to the fire that was among them.
He took up some of it and put it into the hands
of the man in linen,
who took it and went out.

(Under the wings of the *cherubim*
could be seen what looked like the hands of a man.)

I looked . . .
and I saw beside the *cherubim four wheels*,
one beside each of the cherubim;
the *wheels* sparkled like chrysolite.

As for their appearance,
the four of them looked alike;
each was like a wheel intersecting a wheel.

As they moved
they would go in any one of the four directions
the *cherubim* faced
the *wheels* did not turn about as the *cherubim* went.
The *cherubim* went in whatever direction the head faced,
without turning as they went.

Their entire bodies,
including their backs,
their hands and their wings,
were completely full of eyes,
as were their four wheels.

I heard the wheels being called
"the whirling wheels."

Each of the cherubim had four faces:
One face was that of a ***cherub***,
the second the face of a ***man***,
the third the face of a ***lion***,
and the fourth the face of an ***eagle***.

Then the **cherubim** rose upward.
These were the **living creatures**
I had seen by the Kebar River.

When the ***cherubim*** moved,
*the **wheels** beside them moved;*
and when the ***cherubim spread their wings***
to rise from the ground,
the ***wheels*** did not leave their side.

When the ***cherubim*** stood still,
they also stood still;
and when the ***cherubim*** rose,
they rose with them,
**because the Spirit of the living creatures
was in them.**

Then the glory of the LORD
departed from over the threshold of the temple
and stopped above the ***cherubim***.

While I watched,
the cherubim spread their wings
and rose from the ground,
and as they went,
the *wheels* went with them.

They stopped at the entrance
to the east gate of the LORD's house,
and the glory of the God of Israel was above them.

These were the **living creatures**
I had seen beneath the **God of Israel** by the Kebar River,
and I realized that they were **cherubim**.

Each had four faces and four wings,
and under their wings
was what looked like the hands of a man.

Their faces had the same appearance
as those I had seen by the Kebar River.
Each one went straight ahead.

Ezekiel 10:1-22

HERE I AM, SEND ME

I saw the Lord seated on a throne, high and exalted,
and the train of His robe filled the temple.
Above Him were seraphs, each with six wings:
With two wings they covered their faces,
with two they covered their feet, and with two they were flying.
And they were calling to one another:
"Holy, holy, holy is the LORD Almighty;
the whole earth is full of His glory."

At the sound of their voices the doorposts and thresholds shook
and the temple was filled with **smoke**.

"Woe to me!" I cried. "I am ruined!
For I am a man of unclean lips,
and I live among a people of unclean lips,
and my eyes have seen the King, the LORD Almighty."

Then one of the seraphs flew to me
with a live coal in his hand,
which he had taken with tongs from the altar.
With it he touched my mouth and said,
"See, this has touched your lips;
your guilt is taken away and your sin atoned for."

Then I heard the voice of the **Lord** saying,
"Whom shall I send? And who will go for Us?"
And I said, "Here am I. Send me!"

Isaiah 6:1-8

THE ANCIENT OF DAYS

As I looked . . .
***thrones were set in place,
and the Ancient of Days took His seat.***

His ***clothing*** was as white as snow;
the ***hair*** of His head was white like wool.
His ***throne*** *was flaming with fire,* and its ***wheels*** *were all ablaze.*

A river of fire was flowing, coming out from before Him.
Thousands upon thousands attended Him;
ten thousand times ten thousand stood before Him.
The court was seated, and the books were opened.

In my vision at night I looked,
***and there before me was one like a Son of Man,
coming with the clouds of heaven.***

He approached the Ancient of Days
and was led into His presence.
He was given
***authority, glory and sovereign power;
all peoples, nations and men of every language
worshiped Him.***
His dominion is an everlasting dominion
that will not pass away,
and His kingdom is one
that will never be destroyed.

*But the saints of the Most High
will receive the kingdom and will possess it forever— yes,
for ever and ever.*

And as I watched,
this little horn was waging war against the saints
. . . and defeating them,

*until . . . the Ancient of Days came and pronounced judgment
in favor of the saints of the Most High,*
and the time came when they possessed the kingdom.

And though this king will arise, different from the earlier ones;
He will speak against the Most High and oppress His saints
and try to change the set times and the laws.
The saints will be handed over to him
for a time, times and half a time.

But the court will sit,
and his power will be taken away
and completely destroyed forever.

*Then the sovereignty, power and greatness
of the kingdoms under the whole heaven
will be handed over to the saints,
the people of the Most High.*

His kingdom will be an everlasting kingdom,
and all rulers will worship and obey Him.

Daniel 7:9 -10, 13-14, 18, 21-22, 24-27*

THE HEAVENLY MAN IN LINEN

In the third year of Cyrus king of Persia, a revelation was given
to Daniel. Its message was true and it concerned a great war.
The understanding of the message came to him in a vision.

At that time I, Daniel, mourned for three weeks. I ate no choice
food; no meat or wine touched my lips; and I used no lotions
at all until the three weeks were over. As I was standing on the
bank of the great river, the Tigris,

I looked up and there before me was a man dressed in linen,
with a belt of the finest gold around His waist.
His body was like chrysolite,
His face like lightning,
His eyes like flaming torches,
His arms and legs like the gleam of burnished bronze,
and His voice like the sound of a multitude.

I, _____ , was the only one who saw the vision; the men
with me did not see it, but such terror overwhelmed them that
they fled and hid themselves. So I was left alone, gazing at this
great vision; I had no strength left, my face turned deathly pale
and I was helpless.

Then I heard Him speaking, and as I listened to Him,
I fell into a deep sleep, my face to the ground.
A hand touched me
and set me trembling on my hands and knees.

He said, *"_____, you who are highly esteemed,
consider carefully the words I am about to speak to you,
and stand up, for I have now been sent to you."*

And when He said this to me, I stood up trembling.

Then He continued, *"Do not be afraid, _____.*
***Since the first day that you set your mind
to gain understanding and to humble yourself
before your God, your words were heard,
and I have come in response to them.***

But ***the prince*** of the Persian _____ kingdom
resisted Me twenty-one days.
Then Michael, one of ***the chief princes***, came to help Me,
because I was detained there with ***the king of Persia***.

Now I have come to explain to you
what will happen to your people in the future,
for the vision concerns a time yet to come."

While he was saying this to me,
I bowed with my face toward the ground and was speechless.

Then ***one who looked like a man*** touched my lips,
and I opened my mouth and began to speak.
I said to the one standing before me,
*"I am overcome with anguish because of the vision,
my lord, and I am helpless.
How can I, your servant, talk with You, my lord?
My strength is gone and I can hardly breathe."*

Again *the one who looked like a man* touched me
and gave me strength.
"Do not be afraid, O man highly esteemed," He said.
"Peace! Be strong now; be strong."

When He spoke to me, I was strengthened and said,
"Speak, my lord, since you have given me strength."

So He said, *"Do you know why I have come to you?*
Soon I will return to fight against the prince of Persia,
and when I go, the prince of Greece will come;
but first I will tell you what is written in the Book of Truth.

(No one supports me against them except **Michael**, *your* **prince***.*
And in the first year of Darius the Mede,
I took my stand to support and protect him.)

I heard, but I did not understand. So I asked,
"My lord, what will the outcome of all this be?"

He replied, *"Go your way, Daniel,*
because the words are closed up and sealed
until the time of the end.

Many will be purified, made spotless and refined,
but the wicked will continue to be wicked.
None of the wicked will understand,
but those who are wise will understand.

Daniel 10:1-11:1; 12:8-10*

THE GLORIFIED SON OF MAN

I, John,
your brother and companion
in the **suffering**
and **kingdom**
and **patient endurance**
that are ours in Jesus,
was on the island of Patmos because of the word of God
and the testimony of Jesus.

On the Lord's Day I was in the Spirit,
and I heard behind me a loud voice like a trumpet,
which said:

***"Write on a scroll what you see
and send it to the seven churches:***

I turned around to see the voice that was speaking to me.
And when I turned
I saw seven golden lampstands,
and among the lampstands was someone
"like a son of man,"
*dressed in a robe . . . reaching down to His feet
and with a golden sash around His chest.*

*His head and hair were white like wool,
as white as snow,
and His eyes were like blazing fire.*

His feet were like bronze glowing in a furnace,
and His voice was like the sound of rushing waters.

In His right hand He held seven stars,
and out of His mouth . . . came a sharp double-edged sword.
His face was like the sun shining in all its brilliance.

When I saw Him,
I fell at His feet as though dead.

Then He placed his right hand on me and said:

"Do not be afraid.
I am the First and the Last.

I am the Living One;
I was dead,
and behold I am alive . . . for ever and ever!
And I hold the keys of death and Hades.

Revelation 1:9-18

THE HEAVENLY THRONEROOM

After this I looked,
and there before me was a door standing open in heaven.
And the voice I had first heard speaking to me like a trumpet
said, *"Come up here,*
and I will show you what must take place after this.

"At once I was in the Spirit,
and there before me was a throne in heaven
with someone sitting on it.

And the one Who sat there
had the appearance of jasper and carnelian.
A rainbow, resembling an emerald, encircled the throne.

Surrounding the throne were twenty-four other thrones,
and seated on them were twenty-four elders.
They were dressed in white
and had crowns of gold on their heads.

From the throne came flashes of lightning,
rumblings and peals of thunder.
Before the throne, seven lamps were blazing.
These are the seven spirits of God.
Also before the throne there was what looked like
a sea of glass, clear as crystal.

In the center, around the throne, were four living creatures,
and they were covered with eyes, in front and in back.

The first living creature was like a lion,
the second was like an ox,
the third had a face like a man,
the fourth was like a flying eagle.

Each of the four living creatures had six wings
and was covered with eyes all around, even under his wings

Day and night they never stop saying:
"Holy, holy, holy
is the Lord God Almighty,
Who was, and is, and is to come."

Whenever the living creatures give
glory, honor and thanks
to Him who sits on the throne
and Who lives for ever and ever,
the twenty-four elders fall down before Him
Who sits on the throne,
and worship Him Who lives for ever and ever.

They lay their crowns before the throne and say:
"You are worthy, our Lord and God,
*to receive **glory***
*and **honor***
*and **power**,*
for You created all things,
and by Your will they were created and have their being."

Revelation 4:1-11

FAITHFUL AND TRUE

I saw heaven standing open
and there before me was a white horse,
whose rider is called **Faithful** and **True**.
With justice He judges and makes war.

His **eyes** are like **blazing fire**,
and on His **head** are **many crowns**.
He has **a name** written on Him
that no one knows . . . **but He Himself**.

He is dressed in a **robe** dipped in **blood**,
and His **name** is the **Word of God**.

The **armies of heaven** were following Him,
riding **on white horses** and **dressed in fine linen**,
white and clean.

Out of His **mouth** comes a **sharp sword**
with which to strike down the nations.
"He will rule them with an iron scepter."
He treads the winepress of the fury of the wrath of
God Almighty.

On His **robe** and on His **thigh**
He has this name written:
KING OF KINGS AND LORD OF LORDS.

Revelation 19:11-21

69

The Psalm

THE PSALMS

I call to God, and the Lord saves me.
Evening, morning and noon I cry out in distress,
and he hears my voice.

INTRODUCTION TO PRAYING THE PSALMS

Just as the 'Prayers of the Prophets' reveal the feelings of God in his pursuit of man, so the Psalms reveal the feelings of man in his pursuit of God. And David, author of the majority of the Psalms, was an amazing man. He lived in a day when there was no Bible to speak of. Of course, he would have had the first five books of Moses – Genesis, Exodus, Leviticus, Numbers and Deuteronomy – but that would have been about it. Judges would have existed in fragments, and maybe other writings called "The Book of the Wars of the Lord" (Num. 21:14). But beyond that, faith in the One True God came out of an individual or corporate experience with Him. David's experiences – his battles, hardships, and delights in God – became his own salvation history, a salvation history that relates to all mankind. It is incredible to think that, although they were written three thousand years ago, David's pleasures and struggles with God and his fellow man still have relevance to our situations. In fact, David's relationship with God becomes for us, through the Psalms, an example of how we can relate to God today.

David talked to God a lot. And what he talked about was . . . his feelings! He brought God into his boring job in the sheep fields and looked at work as though God had his job (Ps. 23). He told him how he felt about his enemies (Ps. 94). He expressed his passionate love for God in unabashed worship (Ps 27), and his remorse over his wicked heart in deep repentance (Ps. 51). He took all his feelings to God. Written from the perspective of a relatively uncultured tribesman, who eked out an existence living off the land, the Psalms, amazingly, contain some of the loftiest, spiritual prose known to man. To be sure, much of it came by direct revelation and unction (1 Chr. 28:11-12, 19), but a lot of it also came as a result of the way God worked in his life. Inspired in the dim, spiritually charged atmosphere of the Tabernacle, and in the spectacular, mysterious expanse of the Temple, these Psalms were composed and recorded on site. Faithful scribes sat in the corner, quill and leather page in hand, to capture the spontaneous "Song of the Lord." This is how David patched together a book of praise and worship, which eventually became the first musical prayer book in history.

Inspired by God, David set up an elaborate system of worship/praise/prayer that became the pattern ever after (1 Chr 23:27-28, 30; 25:1). In summary the entire system was ". . . prescribed by David and Gad, the king's seer, and Nathan, the prophet; [as] was commanded by the LORD through his prophets" (2 Chr. 29:25). Later, whenever the fallen nation came back to God, and reopened the Temple, the prescribed worship was put back into place "as David commanded." This is the recurring pattern in all the revivals of the Old Testament. Each time there was repentance, the leaders commanded all the people of God to pray the Psalms (see Jehoshaphat - 2 Chr.20, c. 900 B.C.; Hezekiah - 2 Chr. 29 – 30 c. 726 - 725 B.C.; Josiah - 2 Chr. 35, c.

625-623 B.C.; Ezra and Nehemiah - Ezra 3:10-13; Neh. 12:24, c. 450 B.C.)

Thus it was that God used the passionate emotions of David's heart to give expression to what he was searching for in true worship. David was a worshipper and intercessor, *par excellence*. It was said of him that he was "a man after God's own heart." His passion for God was so extraordinary that one might say that Israel's elaborate system of worship, dance, and praise grew out of the devotion of this one man. What David did has never been forgotten by God or man, and today we get to worship with his words. And what are his words about? A simplistic view could break them down into three or four categories. Firstly, the "I love you, I love you, I love you Psalms" of worship and devotion. Secondly, the "I love you and I'm sorry I blew it" Psalms of repentance. And, finally, the "I love you, but I'm in trouble – HELP" Psalms. If we wanted to consider a fourth, it would be the "HELP! Now get'em God" imprecatory Psalms.

Examining these categories in greater detail the historian says, David "appointed some of the Levites to minister before the ark of the LORD, to make petition, to give thanks, and to praise the LORD, the God of Israel" (1 Chr. 16:4). David uses various nuances to describe the larger "I love you, I love you, I love you" dimension of prayer. In this one verse, the four verbs are: *"to minister" (sharath),* meaning "to attend, serve, or wait on;" *"to make petition" (zakar),* which means "to be mindful by recounting and recording, and then causing what is remembered to be continually thought upon;" *"to give thanks" (yadah)* – literally, "to hold out the hand, throw or shoot at or away" – hence, it came to be associated with worship as the extending or throwing up of the hands, to confess or shoot up thanks;" and finally, *"to praise the Lord" (halal),* from which we get hallelujah.

Originally, *"praise"* (*halel*) came from a primitive root word which meant "to be clear of sound, or more usually of color." It eventually metamorphosed into "to shine," whereafter, the word came to be associated with worship and took on the idea of deity-boasting with outrageous celebration. This is how David prescribed worshippers to minister to God. Davidic worship, then, is glorious praise in celebration and devotion.

The second category is the 'I love you and I'm sorry I blew it' - repentance Psalms.' They teach us how to say, "I'm sorry," and, contrary to popular opinion, love does mean having to say you're sorry. Many people need language to articulate the repentance in their hearts. Children also need to learn how to say they're sorry. Since we live in a fallen world, repentance, forgiveness and acceptance are necessary many times during our lifetimes. These Psalms help us to both know how to ask for and receive forgiveness.

Thirdly, the 'Help! Get me outta here Psalms' are prayers for people in crisis. Life is filled with crises, both big and small. David was never too proud to ask for help when he needed it, no matter if he had been good or bad. And he always knew that God would listen and be there for him in all of his many trials. Sometimes he added a thought to these prayers, namely, "as you get me out of here, get them, too!" He gives expression to feelings we all have, but feel guilty articulating. But David prayed such things boldly, because he knew his heart was for God and, therefore, God was on his side. He was asking for justice and he wasn't afraid to pray for it. Although we don't want impure judgements to come back on us, there is a place to "judge righteous judgment" (Jn. 7:24 KJV). And the Psalms of David show us how to do this.

By the NT era, the Psalms were considered the most important of

OT books. The International Standard Bible Encylopaedia says,

> *There has never been any serious question as to the right of the Psalter to a place in the Canon of Scripture. The book is possibly more highly esteemed among Christians than by the Jews. If Christians were permitted to retain only one book in the Old Testament, they would almost certainly choose the Psalms.*
>
> *1*

The NT states that, if you are filled with the Holy Spirit, then praying the Psalms will be a natural outcome (Eph. 5:17-20). All followers of God prayed the Psalms (Acts 2:42; Co. 3:16; James 5:13), and the Church has continued this practice for two thousand years. From the early church onward, all monks and nuns prayed the whole book of Psalms every week. St. Patrick, the famous missionary evangelist to Ireland, was said to recite at least a hundred prayers (Psalms) *a day,* out loud to God. Following his example, the Celtic spiritual iron-men began to pray "the three fifties" daily, that is the entire book of Psalms *every day*. You, too, can now continue this great tradition by beginning to pray the Psalms every day. When they connect with your heart, you will worship 'as David did'. And God will be blessed.

BLESSED IS THE MAN

Blessed is the man
who does not walk in the counsel of the wicked
or stand in the way of sinners
or sit in the seat of mockers.

But his delight is in the law of the LORD,
and on His law he meditates
day and night.

He is like a tree planted by streams of water,
which yields its fruit in season
and whose leaf does not wither.

Whatever he does prospers.

Not so the wicked!

They are like chaff that the wind blows away.
Therefore the wicked will not stand in the judgment,
nor sinners in the assembly of the righteous.

For the LORD
watches over the way of the righteous,
but the way of the wicked will perish.

Psalms 1:1-6

FEARFULLY AND WONDERFULLY MADE

O LORD,
You have searched me and You know me.

You know when I sit and when I rise;
You perceive my thoughts from afar.
You discern my going out and my lying down;
You are familiar with all my ways.

Before a word is on my tongue
You know it completely, *O LORD.*
You hem me in – behind and before;
You have laid Your hand upon me.

Such knowledge is too wonderful for me,
too lofty for me to attain.

Where can I go from Your Spirit?
Where can I flee from Your presence?
If I go up to the heavens,
You are there;
if I make my bed in the depths,
You are there.

If I rise on the wings of the dawn,
if I settle on the far side of the sea,
even there Your hand will guide me,
Your right hand will hold me fast.

If I say, "Surely the darkness will hide me
and the light become night around me,"
even the darkness will not be dark to You;
the night will shine like the day,
for darkness is as light to You.

For You created my inmost being;
You knit me together in my mother's womb.

I praise You because I am fearfully and wonderfully made;
Your works are wonderful, I know that full well.

My frame was not hidden from You
when I was made in the secret place.
When I was woven together in the depths of the earth,
Your eyes saw my unformed body.

All the days ordained for me
were written in Your book
before one of them came to be.

How precious to me are Your thoughts, O God!
How vast is the sum of them!
Were I to count them,
they would outnumber the grains of sand.
When I awake, I am still with You.

If only You would slay the wicked, O God!
Away from me, you bloodthirsty men!
They speak of You with evil intent;
Your adversaries misuse Your name.

Do I not hate those who hate You, O LORD,
and abhor those who rise up against You?
I have nothing but hatred for them;
I count them my enemies.

**Search me, O God,
and know my heart;
test me and know my anxious thoughts.
See if there is any offensive way in me,
and lead me in the way everlasting.**

Psalms 139:1-24

A PRAYER OF REPENTANCE

Have mercy on me, O God,
according to Your unfailing love;
according to Your great compassion blot out my transgressions.
Wash away all my iniquity and cleanse me from my sin.

For I know my transgressions,
and my sin is always before me.

Against You . . . and You only,
have I sinned and done what is evil in Your sight,
so that You are proved right when You speak
and justified when You judge.

Surely I was sinful at birth,
sinful from the time my mother conceived me.
Surely You desire truth in the inner parts;
You teach me wisdom in the inmost place.

Cleanse me with hyssop . . . and I will be clean;
wash me . . . and I will be whiter than snow.
Let me hear joy and gladness;
let the bones You have crushed rejoice.

Hide Your face from my sins
and blot out all my iniquity.

Create in me a pure heart, O God,
and renew a steadfast spirit within me.
Do not cast me from Your presence
or take Your Holy Spirit from me.

Restore to me the joy of your salvation
and grant me a willing spirit, to sustain me.
Then I will teach transgressors Your ways,
and sinners will turn back to You.

Save me from bloodguilt, . . . O God,
the God who saves me,
and my tongue will sing of Your righteousness.

O Lord, open my lips,
and my mouth will declare Your praise.

You do not delight in sacrifice,
or I would bring it;
You do not take pleasure in offerings.

The sacrifices of God . . . are a broken spirit;
a broken and contrite heart,
O God, You will not despise.

In Your good pleasure make *Zion* prosper;
make the *Church* prosper;
build up the walls of *Jerusalem*.

Then there will be *righteous sacrifices*,
and *offerings* to delight You;
then *true worship* will be offered on Your altar.

Psalms 51:1-19 *

SAVE ME OH GOD

Keep me safe, O God, for in You I take refuge.
I said to the LORD,
"You are my Lord; apart from You I have no good thing."
As for the saints who are in the land,
they are the glorious ones in whom is all my delight.
The sorrows of those will increase who run after other gods.
I will not pour out their libations of blood
or take up their names on my lips.

LORD, You have assigned me my portion and my cup;
You have made my lot secure.
The boundary lines have fallen for me in pleasant places;
surely I have a delightful inheritance.
I will praise the LORD, Who counsels me;
even at night my heart instructs me.

I have set the LORD always before me.
Because He is at my right hand, I will not be shaken.

Therefore my heart is glad and my tongue rejoices;
my body also will rest secure,
because You will not abandon me to the grave,
nor will You let your Holy One see decay.

You have made known to me the path of life;
You will fill me with joy in your presence,
with eternal pleasures at Your right hand.

Psalms 16:1-11

84

THE LORD IS MY SHEPHERD

The LORD is my shepherd,
I shall not be in want.

He makes me lie down in *green pastures,*
He leads me beside *quiet waters,*
He restores my soul.

He guides me in paths of righteousness
for His name's sake.

Even though I walk . . . through the valley
of the shadow of death,
I will fear no evil,
for You are with me;
Your rod and Your staff,
they comfort me.

You *prepare a table* before me
in the presence of my enemies.
You anoint my head with oil;
my cup overflows.

Surely goodness and love
will follow me all the days of my life,
and I will dwell in the house of the LORD
. . . forever.

Psalms 23:1-6

BATTLE HYMN OF THE KING

I love You, *O LORD*, my strength.
The *LORD* is my *rock*, my *fortress* and my *deliverer*;
my God is my *rock*, in Whom I take *refuge*.
He is my *shield* and the *horn* of my salvation, my *stronghold*.
I call to the LORD, who is worthy of praise,
and I am saved from my enemies.

The cords of *death* entangled me;
the torrents of *destruction* overwhelmed me.
The cords of the *grave* coiled around me;
the snares of *death* confronted me.

In my distress *I called* to the LORD;
I cried to my God for help.
From His temple *He heard* my voice;
my cry came before Him, into His ears.

The earth trembled and quaked,
and the foundations of the mountains shook;
they trembled . . . because He was angry.

Smoke rose from His nostrils;
consuming fire came from His mouth,
burning coals blazed out of it.
He parted the heavens and came down;
dark clouds were under His feet.
He *mounted the cherubim* and flew;
He *soared* on the wings of the wind.

———

86

He made **darkness** his **covering**,
his canopy around Him – the **dark rain clouds** of the sky.
Out of the **brightness** *of His presence* **clouds** *advanced,*
with **hailstones** and **bolts of lightning**.

The LORD **thundered** from heaven;
the **voice** of the **Most High** resounded.
He shot his **arrows** *and scattered,*
great **bolts of lightning** and routed them.

He reached down from on high and **took hold of me**;
He **drew me out** of deep waters.
He **rescued me** from my powerful enemy,
from my foes, who were too strong for me.

They confronted me in the day of my disaster,
but the LORD was my support.
He brought me out into a spacious place;
He rescued me because He delighted in me.

The LORD has dealt with me according to my righteousness;
according to the cleanness of my hands He has rewarded me.

For I have kept the ways of the LORD;
I have not done evil by turning from my God.
All His laws are before me;
I have not turned away from His decrees.
I have been blameless before Him
and have kept myself from sin.

The LORD has rewarded me according to my righteousness,
according to the cleanness of my hands in His sight.

To the *faithful* You show Yourself *faithful*,
to the *blameless* You show Yourself *blameless*,
to the *pure* You show Yourself *pure*,
but to the *crooked* You show Yourself *shrewd*.
You save the *humble*
but bring low those whose eyes are *haughty*.

You, O LORD, keep my lamp burning;
my God turns my darkness into light.
With Your help I can advance against a troop;
with my God I can scale a wall.

For who is God besides the LORD?
And who is the Rock except our God?
It is God who *arms me with strength*
and makes my way perfect.

He *makes my feet* like the feet of a *deer*;
He enables me to *stand on the heights*.
He *trains my hands* for battle;
my arms can bend a bow of bronze.

You give me your shield of victory,
and Your right hand sustains me;
You stoop down to make me great.
You broaden the path beneath me,
so that my ankles do not turn.

I pursued my enemies and overtook them;
I did not turn back till they were destroyed.
I crushed them so that they could not rise;
they fell beneath my feet.

You armed me with strength for battle;
You made my adversaries bow at my feet.
You made my enemies turn their backs in flight,
and I destroyed my foes.

They cried for help, but there was no one to save them—
to the LORD, but he did not answer.
I beat them as fine as dust borne on the wind;
I poured them out like mud in the streets.

You have made me the head of nations;
people I did not know are subject to me.

The LORD lives!
Praise be to my Rock!
Exalted be God my Savior!

Therefore I will praise You among the nations,
O LORD;
I will sing praises to Your name.

He gives His king great victories;
He shows unfailing kindness to His anointed,
to David and his descendants forever.

Psalms 18:1-14, 16-29, 31-42, 46, 49-50

UNDER THE SHADOW OF HIS WINGS

He who dwells in the shelter of the Most High
will rest in the shadow of the Almighty.

I will say of the LORD,
"He is my refuge and my fortress,
my God, in whom I trust."

Surely He will save you from the fowler's snare
and from the deadly pestilence.

He will cover you with His feathers,
and under His wings you will find refuge;
His faithfulness will be your shield and rampart.

You will not fear the terror of night,
nor the arrow that flies by day,
nor the pestilence that stalks in the darkness,
nor the plague that destroys at midday.

A thousand may fall at your side,
ten thousand at your right hand,
but it will not come near you.

You will only observe with your eyes
and see the punishment of the wicked.

If you make the Most High your dwelling
even the LORD, who is my refuge
then no harm will befall you,
no disaster will come near your tent.

For He will command His angels concerning you
to guard you in all your ways;
they will lift you up in their hands,
so that you will not strike your foot against a stone.

You will tread upon the lion and the cobra;
you will trample the great lion and the serpent.

"Because he loves Me," says the LORD,
"I will rescue him;
I will protect him,
for he acknowledges My name.

He will call upon Me,
and I will answer him;
I will be with him in trouble,
I will deliver him and honor him.

With long life will I satisfy him
and show him My salvation."

Psalms 91:1-16

BETTER IS ONE DAY

How lovely is Your dwelling place,
O LORD Almighty!

My soul yearns, even faints,
for the courts of the LORD;
my heart and my flesh cry out
for the living God.

Even the sparrow has found a home,
and the swallow a nest for herself,
where she may have her young—
a place near your altar,
O LORD Almighty,
my King and my God.

Blessed are those who dwell in Your house;
they are ever praising You.
Selah

Blessed are those whose strength is in You,
who have set their hearts on pilgrimage.

As they pass through the Valley of Baca,
they make it a place of springs;
the autumn rains also cover it with pools.

They go from strength to strength,
till each appears before God in Zion.

Hear my prayer,
O LORD God Almighty;
listen to me, O God of Jacob.
Selah

Look upon our shield, O God;
look with favor on Your anointed one.

Better is one day in Your courts
than a thousand elsewhere;

I would rather be a doorkeeper
in the house of my God
than dwell in the tents of the wicked.

For the LORD God is a sun and shield;
the LORD bestows favor and honor;
no good thing does He withhold
from those whose walk is blameless.

O LORD Almighty,
blessed is the man who trusts in You.

Psalms 84:1-12

JESUS PRAYER FROM THE CROSS

My God, my God,
why have You forsaken me?
Why are You so far from saving me,
so far from the words of my groaning?

O my God, I cry out by day, but You do not answer,
by night, and am not silent.
Yet You are enthroned as the Holy One;
You are the praise of Israel.
In You our fathers put their trust;
they trusted and You delivered them.
They cried to You and were saved;
in You they trusted and were not disappointed.

But I am a worm and not a man,
scorned by men and despised by the people.
All who see me mock me;
they hurl insults, shaking their heads:

"He trusts in the LORD . . . let the LORD rescue him.
Let Him deliver him, since He delights in him."

Yet You brought me out of the womb;
You made me trust in You . . . even at my mother's breast.
From birth I was cast upon You;
from my mother's womb You have been my God.

Do not be far from me,
for trouble is near and there is no one to help.

Many bulls surround me; strong bulls of Bashan encircle me.
Roaring lions tearing their prey
open their mouths wide against me.

I am poured out like water, and all my bones are out of joint.
My heart has turned to wax; it has melted away within me.
My strength is dried up like clay,
and my tongue sticks to the roof of my mouth;
You have laid me . . . in the dust . . . of death.

Dogs have surrounded me;
a band of evil men has encircled me,
they have pierced . . . my hands . . . and my feet.
I can count all my bones; people stare and gloat over me.
They divide my garments among them
and cast lots for my clothing.

But you, O LORD . . . be not far off;
O my Strength, come quickly to help me.
Deliver my life from the sword,
my precious life from the power of the dogs.
Rescue me from the mouth of the lions;
save me from the horns of the wild oxen.

I will declare Your name to my brothers;
in the congregation . . . I will praise You.

You who fear the LORD, praise Him!
All you descendants of Jacob, honor Him!
Revere Him, all you descendants of Israel!

For He has not despised or disdained
the suffering of the afflicted one;
He has not hidden his face from him
but has listened to his cry for help.

From You comes the theme of my praise in the great assembly;
before those who fear You will I fulfill my vows.
The poor will eat and be satisfied;
they who seek the LORD will praise Him—
May your hearts live forever!

All the ends of the earth will remember
and turn to the LORD,
and all the families of the nations
will bow down before Him,
for dominion belongs to the LORD
and He rules over the nations.

All the rich of the earth will feast and worship;
all who go down to the dust will kneel before Him—
those who cannot keep themselves alive.

Posterity will serve Him;
future generations will be told about the Lord.

They will proclaim His righteousness
to a people yet unborn — Why . . . ?
For He has done it!

Psalms 22:1-31

LIFT UP YOUR HEADS

The earth is the LORD's, and everything in it,
the world, and all who live in it;
He founded it upon the seas and established it upon the waters.

Who may ascend the hill of the LORD?
Who may stand in His holy place?
He who has clean hands and a pure heart,
who does not lift up his soul to an idol
or swear by what is false.
He will receive blessing from the LORD
and vindication from God his Savior.
Such is the generation of those who seek Him,
who seek Your face, O God of Jacob.

Lift up your heads, O you gates;
be lifted up, you ancient doors,
that the King of glory may come in.

Who is this King of glory?
The LORD strong and mighty, the LORD mighty in battle.

Lift up your heads, O you gates;
lift them up, you ancient doors,
that the King of glory may come in.

Who is he, this King of glory?
The LORD Almighty — He is the King of glory.

Psalms 24:1-10

A PRAYER FOR LEADERS

May the LORD **answer you** when you are in distress;
may the name of the God of Jacob **protect you.**

May He send **you help** from the sanctuary
and grant **you support** from Zion.
May He **remember** all your sacrifices
and **accept** your burnt offerings. Selah

**May He give you the desire of your heart
and make all your plans succeed.**
We will **shout for joy** when you are victorious
and will **lift up our banners** in the name of our God.

May the LORD grant all your requests.

Now I know that the LORD **saves his anointed**;
He **answers him** from His holy heaven
with the **saving power** of His right hand.

Some trust in chariots and some in horses,
but we trust in the name of the LORD our God.
They are brought to their knees and fall,
but we rise up and stand firm.

**O LORD, save the king!
Answer us when we call!**

Psalms 20:1-9

A BLESSING PSALM OF ACSENTS

Blessed are all who fear the LORD,
who walk in his ways.

You will eat the fruit of your labor;
blessings and prosperity will be yours.

Your wife
will be like a fruitful vine within your house;
your sons
will be like olive shoots around your table.

Thus is the man blessed who fears the LORD.

May the LORD bless you from Zion
all the days of your life;

may you see the prosperity of Jerusalem,
and may you live to see your children's children.

Peace be upon and Israel;
Peace be upon the Church.

Psalms 128:1-6*

Prayers of W

PRAYERS OF WISDOM

*Wisdom calls aloud in the street,
she raises her voice in the public squares.*

INTRODUCTION TO PRAYING THE PRAYERS OF WISDOM

In ancient times, wisdom literature was a common means of helping one live life. Hebrew wisdom literature – Proverbs, Ecclesiastes, and Job – however, has surpassed every form of this *genre* of literature, and remains today the most widely-read writing of its kind. As wisdom literature, its popularity is unrivaled. The sheer brilliance of its work points to supernatural authorship. To this day, its practical applicability to all facets of life renders it a favorite with businessmen, motivational speakers, leaders, parents, and educators of all types. In fact, the wisdom contained in these small books lays at the root of modern western civilization, the English-speaking world, in particular. For instance, in early America, the Proverbs were taught to children in schools across the country, in order to instill in them a strong work ethic and a basis for morality. Even today, principled men and women apply it to their daily lives and are successful because of it. Simply put, praying wisdom prayers will help you live life well, for it was for this purpose that they were written.

The aim of Prayers of Wisdom is laid out in the first verses of Proverbs.

The proverbs of Solomon son of David, king of Israel:

for attaining wisdom and discipline;
for understanding words of insight;
for acquiring a disciplined and prudent life,
doing what is right and just and fair;
for giving prudence to the simple,
knowledge and discretion to the young (Prov. 1:1-4).

Here you see that wisdom is understood as the proper application of spirituality to daily life. Once you have had your head in the heavenlies, praying the *theophanies*, with its clouds, thunders and visions of the throne room, how do you walk when your feet hit the ground? The answer found in Prayers of Wisdom is simple. Among other things, don't be lazy, do not tarry long at the wine, love your wife, and remember God in all that you do. These are the things that will make you a wise son and a good father, or a wholesome daughter and a noble wife.

In this *Book of Prayers*, the wisdom prayers have been arranged topically and deal with ordinary subjects such as wisdom, work, speech, sex and adultery, mercy, virtue, leadership, relationships, and spirituality. These prayers connect with the concerns that all of us have. Who amongst us could not use divine help with these things here on earth? By applying the wisdom found in these prayers, we avoid the many pitfalls of life, thereby saving ourselves from much distress.

I happened to stumble upon the Proverbs during one of the most confusing times of my life. I was in university and having a difficult time reconciling my relatively new faith with all that I was being taught in class. Often I found myself full of doubt, bewildered by all the data coming at me. It was at this point in my life that I 'discovered' the wisdom prayers. A preacher had said that there was a chapter of Proverbs for every day of the month, and that it would be wise to read one a day. Armed with this new piece of advice, I launched out and began to read them in my customary fashion – praying each Proverb slowly, word by word. As I faithfully prayed through them day after day, the wisdom theme stuck out. I became intrigued with the whole concept. Wisdom was, the Bible said, "more profitable than silver . . . gold . . . and rubies; nothing [I could] desire compared with her" (Prov. 3:13-15).

This thought set me on a quest for wisdom. I combed the Scriptures for every reference I could find. In the end, I came back to where I started and found that "the fear of the LORD is the beginning of wisdom, and knowledge of the Holy One is understanding" (Prov 9:10). I continued to pray the Proverbs every day for months on end, and eventually came out of my confusion. By the end of my time at university, in certain ways, I was "wiser than my enemies . . . I had more insight than all my teachers, for I meditated on your statutes" (Psalm 119:99). Praying Prayers of Wisdom will make a tangible difference in our daily lives.

We recommend praying all the practical topics found in this section. Children and teenagers, especially, should be praying for this divine wisdom daily, since they are growing up in a culture increasingly contrary to these wise ways. Your daily life will improve significantly if you pray them repeatedly until they are impressed upon your heart.

A TIME FOR EVERYTHING

There is a time for everything,
and a season for every activity under heaven:

*a time to be **born** and a time to **die**,*
*a time to **plant** and a time to **uproot**,*
*a time to **kill** and a time to **heal**,*
*a time to **tear down** and a time to **build**,*
*a time to **weep** and a time to **laugh**,*
*a time to **mourn** and a time to **dance**,*
*a time to **scatter stones** and a time to **gather them**,*
*a time to **embrace** and a time to **refrain**,*
*a time to **search** and a time to **give up**,*
*a time to **keep** and a time to **throw away**,*
*a time to **tear** and a time to **mend**,*
*a time to be **silent** and a time to **speak**,*
*a time to **love** and a time to **hate**,*
*a time for **war** and a time for **peace**.*

God has made everything beautiful in its time.
He has also set eternity in the hearts of men;
yet they cannot fathom what God has done
from beginning to end.

Ecclesiastes 3:1-8, 11

WISDOM CALLS OUT

Lord, You have said,
My son, if you accept my words
and store up my commands within you,
turning your ear to wisdom
and applying your heart to understanding,
and if you call out for insight
and cry aloud for understanding,
and if you look for it as for silver
and search for it as for hidden treasure,
then you will understand the fear of the LORD
and find the knowledge of God.
For the LORD gives wisdom,
and from his mouth come knowledge and understanding.

Father, I ask for this heart of wisdom, and I believe:
The fear of the LORD is the beginning of wisdom,
and knowledge of the Holy One is understanding.
Through them my days will be many,
and years will be added to my life.

So I say to wisdom, "You are my sister,"
and I call understanding "my kinsman."
I will apply my heart to instruction
and my ears to words of knowledge.

Wisdom is supreme; therefore I will get wisdom.
Though it cost me all I have, I will get understanding.

Proverbs 2:1-6; 9:9-10; 7:4; 23:12; 4:7*

THE RIGHTEOUS WORKMAN

As I went past the field of the sluggard,
past the vineyard of the man who lacks judgment;
thorns had come up everywhere, weeds covered the ground.
I applied my heart to what I observed and learned a lesson
from what I saw: A little sleep, a little slumber,
a little folding of the hands to rest – and poverty
will come on you like a bandit and scarcity like an armed man.

Lord you have said,
that I am not to wear myself out to get rich;
but to have wisdom and show restraint.
Yet, you have also said; All hard work brings a profit,
but mere talk leads only to poverty.

I ask you . . . help me to be a wise son.
For lazy hands make a man poor,
but diligent hands bring wealth.
And he who gathers crops in summer is a wise son,
but he who sleeps during harvest is a disgraceful son.
Deliver me from the sins and excuses of the sluggard who says,
"There is a lion in the road, a fierce lion roaming the streets!
So as a door turns on its hinges, I'll just turn on my bed."

For the one who is slack in his work
is brother to him that is a great waster.
As you have said, Show me a man skilled in his work?
He will stand before kings; not before obscure men.

Proverbs 24:30-34; 23:4; 14:23; 10:4-5;
26:13-14; 18:9; 22:29*

LET MY WORDS BE FEW

I will watch my ways and keep my tongue from sin;
I will put a muzzle on my mouth
as long as the wicked are in my presence.

Father, help me to guard my lips because
he who guards his lips guards his life,
but he who speaks rashly will come to ruin.
For life and death are in the power of the tongue,
and reckless words pierce like a sword,
but the tongue of the wise brings healing.
And when words are many, sin is not absent,
but the one who holds his tongue is wise.

Give me the gentle answer that turns away wrath,
instead of a harsh word that stirs up anger.
For it is to a man's honor to avoid strife,
but every fool is quick to quarrel;
and a fool shows his annoyance at once,
but a prudent man overlooks an insult.

Lord . . . grow the fruit of self control in my life,
for through patience even a ruler can be persuaded,
and a gentle tongue can break a bone.
I will not be quick with my mouth,
For you, oh God, are in heaven . . . and I am on earth,
so I will let my words be few.

Psalms 39:1; Proverbs 13:3; 18:21; 12:18;
10:19; 15:1; 12:16; 20:3; 25:15; Ecclesiastes 5:2*

DELIVER ME FROM EVIL

I have made a covenant with my eyes
not to look lustfully at a girl.
For You oh Lord, see my ways . . . and count my every step.
Father I ask, that you keep me from the immoral woman,
from the smooth tongue of the wayward wife.
Do not let me lust in my heart after her beauty
or let her captivate me with her eyes;
for the prostitute reduces a man to a loaf of bread,
and the adulteress preys upon your very life.
Can a man take fire into his lap without being burned?
So is he who sleeps with another man's wife;
no one who touches her will go unpunished.
And this is the way of an adulteress: She eats
and wipes her mouth and says, 'I've done nothing wrong.'
But you say, a man who commits adultery lacks judgment;
and whoever does, his shame will never be wiped away;
for her house leads down to death.
None who go to her return or attain the paths of life.

So I will drink water from my own cistern,
running water from my own well.
I will rejoice in the wife of my youth.
As a loving doe, a graceful deer – may her breasts satisfy me
always, Let me ever be captivated by her love.
For I know that my ways are in full view of you, oh LORD,
and you examine all my paths.

Job 31:1;Proverbs 6:24-27,29; 30:20; 6:32-33; 2:18-19;
5:15-21*

MERCY

Father in Heaven, you have said . . .
He who oppresses the poor shows contempt for their Maker,
but whoever is kind to the needy honors God.
For rich and poor have this in common:
The LORD is the Maker of them all.
So I will not exploit the poor because they are poor
nor crush the needy in court, for you will take up their case
and will plunder those who plunder them.

The righteous care about justice for the poor,
but the wicked have no such concern.
And you say, he who is kind to the poor lends to the LORD,
and the LORD he will reward him for what he has done.

Let me be like Job, who said:
I rescued the poor who cried for help,
and the fatherless who had none to assist him.
The man who was dying blessed me;
I made the widow's heart sing.
I was eyes to the blind and feet to the lame.
I was a father to the needy; I took up the case of the stranger.
I broke the fangs of the wicked
and snatched the victims from their teeth.
I chose the way for them and sat as their chief;
I dwelt as a king among his troops;
I was like one who comforts mourners.

Proverbs 14:31; 22:2, 22-23; 29:7; 19:17; 11:25; Job 29:12
−17, 25*

VIRTUE AND HONOR

Father, my prayer is that I will pay attention to what you say,
and listen closely to your words.
For they are life to those who find them
and health to a man's whole body.
Above all else, I will guard my heart, it is the wellspring of life.
For he who pursues righteousness and love
finds life, prosperity and honor.

I will put away perversity from my mouth,
and keep corrupt talk far from my lips.
I will make level paths for my feet,
and take only ways that are firm.
For a good name is more desirable than great riches;
to be esteemed is better than silver or gold.

Lord, I will honor you with my wealth,
with the firstfruits of all my crops;
then, as you have said, my barns will be filled to overflowing,
and my vats will brim over with new wine.

Help me to walk with the wise,
for he who walks with the wise grows wise,
but a companion of fools suffers harm.
I will not be misled: ***"Bad company corrupts good character."***
But the fear of the LORD adds length to life,
whereas, the years of the wicked are cut short.

Proverbs 4:20, 22-23; 21:21; 4:24, 26;22:1;
3:9-10; 13:20; 1 Cor. 15:33: Prov. 10:27*

THE WAY OF A KING

There are three things that are stately in their stride,
four that move with stately bearing:
a lion, mighty among beasts, who retreats before nothing;
a strutting rooster, a he-goat, and a **king with his army**.

Father, you say that it is the glory of God to conceal a matter,
but to search out a matter is the glory of kings.
So I ask for the wisdom to search out your ways,
for by wisdom kings reign and rulers make laws that are just;
and by it princes govern, and all nobles who rule on earth.
For it is better to be a poor but wise youth than
an old but foolish king who no longer takes warning.

I ask for a heart to rule justly
For by justice a king gives a country stability,
and if a king judges the poor with fairness,
his throne will always be secure.

I pray also for kingly character, for as you say,
O my son, O son of my womb, O son of my vows,
do not spend your strength on women,
your vigor on those who ruin kings.
It is not for kings, – not for kings to drink wine, not for rulers to
crave beer, lest they drink and forget what the law decrees,
and deprive all the oppressed of their rights.
I will speak up for those who cannot speak for themselves,
for the rights of all who are destitute.

Pr. 30:29-31; 25:2; 8:15-16; Eccl. 4:13; Pr. 29:4, 14; 31:2-8*

IN PRAISE OF THE NOBLE WIFE

A wife of noble character who can find?
She is worth far more than rubies.
Her husband has full confidence in her and lacks nothing.
She brings him good, not harm, all the days of her life.
She is like the merchant ships, bringing her food from afar.
She gets up while it is still dark;
she provides food for her family and portions for her servant girls.
She considers a field and buys it;
she plants a vineyard out of her earnings.
She sets about her work vigorusly, she is strong for her tasks.
She sees that her trading is profitable,
and her lamp does not go out at night.
She opens her arms to the poor and extends her hands to the needy.

Her husband is respected at the city gate,
where he takes his seat among the elders of the land.
She is clothed with strength and dignity;
she can laugh at the days to come.
She speaks with wisdom, and faithful instruction is on her tongue.
She watches over the affairs of her household
and does not eat the bread of idleness.

Her children arise and call her blessed;
her husband also, and he praises her:
"Many women do noble things, but you surpass them all."
Charm is deceptive, and beauty is fleeting;
but a woman who fears the LORD is to be praised.
Give her the reward she has earned,
and let her works bring her praise at the city gate.

Proverbs 31:10 –12, 14-18, 20, 23, 25-31

THE WHOLE DUTY OF MAN

Lord, you have said:
Remember your Creator in the days of your youth,
before the days of trouble come
and the years approach when you will say,
"I find no pleasure in them"—
before the sun and the light and the moon grow dark,
when the keepers of the house tremble, and the strong men
stoop, when the grinders cease because they are few,
and those looking through the windows grow dim;
when men rise up at the sound of birds,
but all their songs grow faint;
when men are afraid of heights and of dangers in the streets;
and the grasshopper drags himself along
and desire no longer is stirred.
Then man goes to his eternal home
and mourners go about the streets.

Remember him – before the silver cord is severed,
or the golden bowl is broken;
and the dust returns to the ground it came from,
and the spirit returns to God who gave it.

Now all has been heard; here is the conclusion of the matter:
Fear God and keep his commandments,
for this is the whole duty of man.
For God will bring every deed into judgment,
including every hidden thing, whether it is good or evil.

Ecclesiastes 12:1-7, 13-14*

Song of Song

THE SONG OF SONGS

Love is as strong as death, its jealousy unyielding as the grave. It burns like blazing fire, like a mighty flame.

INTRODUCTION TO PRAYING THE SONG OF SONGS

It is a big jump to move from praying to "*Abba* Father" to praying directly to the "*Bridegroom.*" Intimacy with the Father looks very different than intimacy with the *Lover.* I well remember, many years ago, my first attempt to pray the Song of Songs. I found myself immediately aware that I was over my head. I was trying to be faithful to the text, but embarrassed to be talking to God in such graphic terms. In the end, blushing, I told the Lord that I could not continue unless He helped me figure out what I was even talking about.

Many people meet with similar problems in their initial endeavors to pray the Song of Songs. How does one deal with all the sexual imagery? Why is this book even in the Bible? Still more confusing is knowing how to approach this book in prayer. To start with, a distinction must be made between its literal and allegorical interpretations, understanding that it certainly conveys both dimensions to the reader. The historical/literal approach maintains that the relationship described is a real one between Solomon and a poor Shulamite woman and through it the purity, beauty and satisfaction of marital love can be seen. The tone is clearly erotic, but it is *eros* undefiled. As such, it sets the standard for human love as God Himself created and intended it to be.

The allegorical interpretation, on the other hand, would be that the Song of Songs depicts the figurative relationship between Jehovah/Jesus (as Lover and Bridegroom) and Israel/ the Church (as his Beloved Bride). This is the approach most often taken by Jews and Christians throughout the ages.

> *. . . the favorite image used for portraying the relationship between Jehovah and His chosen people is that of marriage. Jehovah is the Spouse, Israel the Bride, and the Temple is the house where the conjugal relations, always spiritual in nature, take place. This image is fully developed by Hosea and Ezekiel; but as early as Exodus, Jehovah appears to Israel as a jealous God, and in the books of the prophets, the commission of sin, especially the sin of idolatry, is called infidelity or adultery. In the Gospel the Kingdom of Heaven is on several occasions compared to a wedding feast. St. Paul says he betrothed the Corinthians to the Spouse, Christ, and St. John in the Apocalypse gives us the image of the Lamb with Jerusalem His Bride.[1]*

All of this imagery culminates in the Ephesians passage, where the mystical relationship between Christ and His Church is compared to the physical union of marriage. "For this reason a man shall leave his father and mother and shall be joined to his wife, and the two shall become one flesh. This mystery is great; but *I am speaking with reference to Christ and the church."* (Ephesians 5:31-32 NASB). Here Paul is using marriage as an allegory of spiritual union with God. In this way, he legitimizes using physical love in an allegorical fashion. Therefore, at some point, every serious believer will learn to commune with God in an intensely intimate love relationship. This is where everyone in the Church is heading, as evidenced by the bridal theme in the Book of Revelation. As Ezekiel saw in his vision of water flowing from the Temple, the river of God really is too deep to ford. We just have to get to the point where we are willing for God to hold us by the hand and take us out over our heads, for it is in the deep waters where we become immersed in the beauty of who He is.

An explanation of how to pray this book is needed because the symbolism is difficult to define. The book is, of course, interactive, meaning that it contains antiphonal conversations and scenes between the Lover and the Beloved (and their Friends). Therefore, when praying the Song of Songs, one must first of all put oneself in a posture not only to speak to God, but also to receive from him. Much of this book is God speaking his love over us, so we must be able to *see* and *hear* in the Spirit the face and voice of the Lover. It is essential to believe the words of love that God says about us, or they will not "profit us because they are not mixed with faith" (Hebrews 4:2). For some, this will be the first hurdle to cross in praying the Song of Songs.

How should a person start to pray the Song of Songs? It is good to begin by speaking the words of the Song out loud. These words will expand one's prayer vocabulary to words of intimacy versus theology. They give language to the feelings of the heart through imagery and symbolism, and will lead the intercessor to visualize the Lover, Christ, because they are so descriptive. Mental images of the face of Christ are encouraged so that there is actual interaction with the Person depicted in the text. The words connote an image that helps to convey a thought. In the

Song of Songs, the depiction of erotic love is meant to bring us to the understanding of the progression of the spiritual life unto union. The Lover is Christ, the Bridegroom, and the Beloved is the Church (generally), or the person praying (specifically). The word picture begins to carry us into His presence and adds spice to the otherwise abstract or theological texts of Scripture. God is, after all, love. Then, as we pray through his attributes, symbolically described in the language of love, we will "see" his face in different ways as the Spirit highlights them in our hearts and minds.

What follows is a possible portrayal of how one might enter into The Song of Songs in prayer. We have chosen chapter 4, verses 1 and following from the NKJV to give a brief example of the imagery of the book. First start with the understanding that you are the Beloved and you are listening with your heart to the words of your Lover. You listen while he speaks directly to you: *"Behold, you are fair my love! Behold you are fair!"* Since you have learned the 'love language', you immediately know that the Father and the Son are telling you that you are cleansed, loved and accepted; that you are his Bride and chosen one; that you are special to him. Then as you continue to verbalize what the Lover is saying about you, your Bridegroom (Lover) and you dialogue using a 'secret love language'. He says, *"you have dove's eyes"* (eyes that are devoted and focused on Him). *"Behind your veil"* (your heart/thoughts preserved only for your lover), *"your hair"* (the symbol of your glory) *"is like a flock of goats coming down from Mount Gilead"* (symbol of beauty).[2]

You listen as He goes on to say about you:

"Your teeth" (your smile and presence), *are perfect"* (purified), *"your lips and mouth are lovely"* (your love and words that spring from the abundance of your heart), *"are beautiful and*

beckoning. Your temples behind your veil" (your thoughts and secret desires that you think for the Lord, are sweet, sweet as a piece of pomegranate. V. 9 Oh, he says), *"You have ravished my heart"* (I am captured with love for you; by) *"just one look"* (simply because you have sought me and loved me. I am crazy about you)!

After hearing how the Lover feels about you, you begin to respond and tell him how much you love him. In time, a single phrase from this special love language, either from him to you or from you to him, will be enough to take you into the place of close communion. Included below are some more examples of possible allegorical interpretations so that you may have a greater understanding of the symbolism of the text.

Songs 4:1-3, 9-13 NKJV
The Lover (God/Jesus):

v. 1 *"Behold, you are fair* (cleansed, purified, lovely, accepted) *my love* (my Bride, my chosen, my elect)! *Behold, you are fair! You have dove's eyes* (devoted eyes, a heart focused on Me). *Behind your veil* (modesty, you have been preserved for me…your lover) *your hair* (glory, inheritance) *is like a flock of goats* (picture of her beauty), *going down from Mount Gilead* (rich pastures, strong, powerful).

v. 2 *Your teeth* (smile, presence) *are like a flock of shorn sheep which have come up from the washing* (perfect, purified), *every one of which bears twins, and none is barren among them* (perfection, productive).

v. 3 *Your lips* (love, kisses) *are like a strand of scarlet, and your mouth is lovely* (beautiful, alluring, beckoning). *Your temples behind your veil* (thoughts, secret desires) *are like a piece of pomegranate* (sweet, precious).

v. 9 *You have ravished* (captured, taken, possessed) *my*

heart, my sister, my spouse (my intimate lover, now my family); *you have ravished my heart with one look* (seeking) *of your eyes* (seeking me)*, with one link of your necklace.*

v. 10 *How fair* (good, holy, accepted) *is your love, my sister, my spouse! How much better than wine is your love* (He enjoys her love even more than the pleasures and highs of the world, and she enjoys Him, cf. v.1:5)*, and the scent of your perfumes* (incense, prayers) *than all spices!*

v. 11 *Your lips* (kisses, words, intercession)*, O my spouse, drip as the honeycomb; honey* (sweetness) *and milk* (softness) *are under your tongue; and the fragrance of your garments is like the fragrance of Lebanon* (rich, powerfully wonderful)*.*

v. 12 *A garden enclosed* (reserved for the Jealous One, private) *is my sister, my spouse* (my lover, my Bride, my chosen, my called)*, a spring shut up* (preserved for her lover), *a fountain sealed* (faithful, a virgin, devoted)*.*

v. 13 *Your plants* (intimate love) *are an orchard of pomegranates* (sweet, pleasure-filled) *with pleasant fruits* (spiritual growth)*.*

As you can see, when prayed as a love story, the allegory is rich and meaningful, but it takes time and study to comprehend. We recommend that you search out a few of the great saints throughout history who have brought the subtleties of this book to life. A modern day champion of the allegorical prayer method is Mike Bickle. For over fifteen years he has collected and studied every commentary written on the subject so as to turn it into prayer. For those of you who want help, a great starting place would be to get "The Fire of Love," a devotional prayer CD prayed by Mike Bickle, which models praying the Song of Songs from a bridal perspective (see prayer resource appendix at back). You might also check his web-site (www.fotb.com) for descriptive notes on every word of this beautiful Song. Learn the love language and begin.

Love is as strong as death, its jealousy
unyielding as the grave. It burns like blazing fire,
like a mighty flame.

BEGINNINGS OF INTIMACY AND REVELATION

BELOVED
Kiss me with the kisses of Your mouth
for Your love is more delightful than wine.
Pleasing is the fragrance of Your perfumes;
Your name is like perfume poured out.
No wonder the maidens love You!

Take me away with You – let's hurry!
Let the king , bring me into His chambers.

FRIENDS
We rejoice and delight in You;
we will praise Your love more than wine.

THE BELOVED
How right they are to adore You!
Dark am I, yet lovely, O daughters of Jerusalem,
dark like the tents of Kedar, like the tent curtains of Solomon.

Do not stare at me because I am dark, darkened by the sun.
My mother's sons were angry with me
and made me take care of the vineyards;
my own vineyard I have neglected.

Tell me, You whom I love, where You graze Your flock
Why should I be like a veiled woman
beside the flocks of Your friends?

Song 1:2-7

FAINT WITH LOVE

LOVER
How beautiful you are, my darling!
Oh, how beautiful! Your eyes are doves.

BELOVED
How handsome You are, my lover!
Oh, how charming! And our bed is verdant.

LOVER
The beams of our house are cedars; our rafters are firs.
BELOVED
I am a Rose of Sharon, a lily of the valleys
LOVER
Like a lily among thorns is my darling among the maidens
BELOVED
Like an apple tree among the trees of the forest
is my Lover among the young men.
I delight to sit in His shade, and His fruit is sweet to my taste.
He has taken me to the banquet hall,
and His banner over me is love.

Strengthen me with raisins, refresh me with apples,
for I am faint with love.
His left arm is under my head, and His right arm embraces me.
Daughters of Jerusalem, I charge you
by the gazelles and by the does of the field:
Do not arouse or awaken love until it so desires.

Song 1:15 - 2:7

127

EMBRACING THE LOVERS COMING

BELOVED
Listen! My Lover! Look!

Here He comes, leaping across the mountains,
bounding over the hills.

My Lover is like a gazelle or a young stag.
Look! There He stands behind our wall,
gazing through the windows,
peering through the lattice.

My Lover spoke and said to me,
"Arise, my darling,
my beautiful one, and come with me.

See!
The winter is past;
the rains are over and gone.
Flowers appear on the earth;
the season of singing has come,
the cooing of doves is heard in our land.
The fig tree forms its early fruit;
the blossoming vines spread their fragrance.

Arise, come, my darling;
my beautiful one, come with me.

LOVER
My dove in the clefts of the rock,
in the hiding places on the mountainside,
show me your face,
let me hear your voice;
for your voice is sweet, and your face is lovely.

Catch for us the foxes,
the little foxes that ruin the vineyards,
our vineyards that are in bloom.

BELOVED
My Lover is mine and I am His*;*
He browses among the lilies.
Until the day breaks and the shadows flee,
turn, my Lover,
and be like a gazelle, or like a young stag
on the rugged hills.

Song 2:8-17

THE DARK NIGHT OF LOVE

BELOVED
All night long on my bed
I looked for the One my heart loves;
I looked for Him but did not find Him.

I will get up now and go about the city,
through its streets and squares;
I will search for the One my heart loves.
So I looked for Him but did not find Him.

The watchmen found me
as they made their rounds in the city.
"Have you seen the One my heart loves?"

Scarcely had I passed them
when I found the One my heart loves.
I held Him and would not let Him go
till I had brought Him to my mother's house,
to the room of the one who conceived me.

Daughters of Jerusalem,
I charge you
by the gazelles and by the does of the field:
Do not awaken or arouse love
until it so desires.

Song 3:1-5

THE MIGHT OF THE LOVER

BELOVED
Who is this coming up from the desert
like a column of smoke,
perfumed with myrrh and incense
made from all the spices of the merchant?

Look!
It is Solomon's carriage,
escorted by sixty warriors,
the noblest of Israel,
all of them wearing the sword,
all experienced in battle,
each with his sword at his side,
prepared for the terrors of the night.

King Solomon made for himself the carriage;
he made it of wood from Lebanon.
Its posts he made of silver,
its base of gold.
Its seat was upholstered with purple,
its interior lovingly inlaid by the daughters of Jerusalem.

Come out, you daughters of Zion,
and look at King Solomon wearing the crown,
the crown with which His mother crowned Him
on the day of His wedding,
the day His heart rejoiced.

Song 3:6-11

THE BEAUTY OF THE BELOVED

LOVER
All beautiful you are, my darling;
there is no flaw in you.
Come with me from Lebanon, my bride, come with me.
Descend from the summit of Hermon,
from the lions' dens and the mountain haunts of the leopards.

You have stolen my heart, my sister, my bride;
you have stolen my heart with one glance of your eyes,
with one jewel of your necklace.
How delightful is your love,
my sister, my bride!
How much more pleasing is your love than wine,
and the fragrance of your perfume than any spice!
Your lips drop sweetness as the honeycomb, my bride;
milk and honey are under your tongue.

The fragrance of your garments is like that of Lebanon.
You are a garden locked up, my sister, my bride;
you are a spring enclosed, a sealed fountain.
You are a garden fountain,
a well of flowing water streaming down from Lebanon.

BELOVED
Awake, north wind, and come, south wind!
Blow on my garden, that its fragrance may spread abroad.
Let my lover come into his garden and taste its choice fruits.

Song 4:7-12; 15-16

ANTICIPATION

BELOVED
I slept but my heart was awake.
Listen! My Lover is knocking:
He said **"Open to me, my sister, my darling, my dove,**
my flawless one.
My head is drenched with dew,
my hair with the dampness of the night."

I have taken off my robe – must I put it on again?
I have washed my feet – must I soil them again?
My Lover thrust his hand through the latch-opening;
my heart began to pound for Him.

I arose to open for my Lover, my hands dripped with myrrh,
my fingers with flowing myrrh, on the handles of the lock.
I opened for my Lover, but my Lover had left;
He was gone.

My heart sank at his departure. I looked for Him.
but did not find Him. I called him but He did not answer.
The watchmen found me as they made their rounds in the city.
They beat me, they bruised me; they took away my cloak,
those watchmen of the walls!

O daughters of Jerusalem,
I charge you if you find my Lover, what will you tell Him?
Tell Him I am faint with love.

Song 5:2-8

ALTOGETHER LOVELY

FRIENDS
How is your Beloved better than others,
most beautiful of women?
How is your Beloved better than others,
that you charge us so?

BELOVED
My Lover is radiant and ruddy,
outstanding among ten thousand.

His head is purest gold;
His hair is wavy and black as a raven.
His eyes are like doves by the water streams,
washed in milk, mounted like jewels.
His cheeks are like beds of spice yielding perfume.
His lips are like lilies dripping with myrrh.

His arms are rods of gold set with chrysolite.
His body is like polished ivory decorated with sapphires.
His legs are pillars of marble set on bases of pure gold.
His appearance is like Lebanon, choice as its cedars.
His mouth is sweetness itself;
He is altogether lovely.

This is my Lover, this my Friend,
O daughters of Jerusalem.

Song 5:9-16

THE RAVISHED BRIDEGROOM

LOVER
You are beautiful, my darling, as Tirzah,
lovely as Jerusalem, majestic as troops with banners.
Turn your eyes from me; they overwhelm me.

Your hair is like a flock of goats descending from Gilead.
Your teeth are like a flock of sheep coming from the washing.
Each has its twin, not one of them is alone.

Your temples behind your veil are like pomegranates.
Sixty queens there may be, and eighty concubines,
and virgins beyond number;
but my dove . . . my perfect one . . . is unique,
only daughter of her mother, favorite of the one who bore her.
The maidens saw her and called her blessed;
the queens and concubines praised her.

FRIENDS
Who is this that appears like the dawn, fair as the moon,
bright as the sun, majestic as the stars in procession?
Come back, come back, O Shulammite;
come back, come back, that we may gaze on you!

LOVER
Why would you gaze on the Shulammite
as on the dance of Mahanaim?

Song 6:4-10; 13

THE BRIDAL SEAL OF DIVINE FIRE

FRIENDS
Who is this coming up from the desert leaning on her lover?
LOVER
Under the apple tree I roused you;
there your mother conceived you,
there she who was in labor gave you birth.

Place me like a seal over your heart,
like a seal on your arm; for love is as strong as death,
its jealousy unyielding as the grave.
It burns like blazing fire, like a mighty flame.
Many waters cannot quench love; rivers cannot wash it away.
If one were to give all the wealth of his house for love,
it would be utterly scorned.

BELOVED
My own vineyard is mine to give;
the thousand shekels are for you, O Solomon,
and two hundred are for those who tend its fruit
LOVER
You who dwell in the gardens with friends in attendance,
let me hear your voice!

BELOVED
Come away, my lover,
and be like a gazelle or like a young stag
on the spice-laden mountains.

Song 8:5-7; 12-14

Prayers of the Prophets

PRAYERS OF THE PROPHETS

Because your sins are so many and your hostility so great, the prophet is considered a fool, the inspired man a maniac.

INTRODUCTION TO PRAYING THE PRAYERS OF THE PROPHETS

Praying the prayers of the prophets opens up realms not usually touched in prayer. In them, more than in any other of the biblical texts, you enter the feelings of God. It is the prophets who display, in both their lifestyles and their language, the passionate emotions of the One who made us all. I have heard many people who pray about knowing the heart of God. If that has ever been your desire – that you know the heart of God – then praying the prophets will be your place of discovery. The prophets seem to be not only allowed, but required by God, to enter into the fellowship of His sufferings (Phil. 3:10). They are asked to feel what He feels and then to declare it to the rest of us. Think of Hosea – his whole lifestyle spoke of the suffering that a jealous God endures generation after generation. Or Ezekiel, whose wife dies overnight and Ezekiel is not even allowed to mourn as a sign to the people (Ezekiel 24:15-24). Jeremiah wishes his *"head were waters and his eyes a fountain of tears"* (Jeremiah 9:1) so that he could weep day and night for the slain daughter of his people. No doubt about it – God is a passionate Person.

He doesn't reside in a cranium, but in the emotions and pain of every day life. If he weren't so lovesick, our sins and idolatries would not hurt so much. But the prophets reveal that God has pain and anger, as well as pleasure and delight. And God allows his servants, the prophets, to enter into his heart in a way many of us never even dream of. By praying the prayers of the prophets, we see not only the human suffering that comes from rejecting his love, but also the divine suffering of being rejected . . ."*How I [God speaking] have been hurt by their adulterous hearts which have turned away from me.*" *(Ezekiel 6:9 NASB).*

The prophets' section of the Bible is massive. In truth, all the biblical writers were prophets, including Moses (who wrote the Law), and David (who wrote the Psalms). They *saw* in the spirit; they *heard* the voice of God. Then they simply announced it. There are many more prayers of the prophets than are included here, and this brief selection only attempts to touch on the various cross sections of life. For example, Job said, "Man is born to trouble as surely as sparks fly upward (Job 5:7)." When in trouble, most people lose all ability to pray anything other than "HELP!" But the Prayers of the Prophets, like the Psalms, are the stuff that life is really made of. They express the deep emotions of war, death, thankfulness, confusion, judgement and blessing. Unlike Jabez, most people are afraid to cry boldly: "Oh, that You would bless me indeed, and enlarge my territory (1 Chron. 4:10)." In times of crisis, we often have difficulty knowing what to pray when there are real enemies, armies or terrorists. But we find prayers in the prophets that help in such times. King Jehoshaphat was able to pray with integrity "O our God, will You not judge them? For we have no power to face this vast army that is attacking us. We do not know what to do, but our eyes are upon You (2 Chron. 20:12)." What do we do with the many imprecatory prayers of the prophets? We pray them!

Western Christianity tries to sterilize the Bible and religion. The prophets don't know anything of this. They call the proverbial spade – a spade, and they pray that way too. The way to pray the prayers of the prophets is to apply their problems and situations to your problems and situations. When you are going through something, find a prayer that is readily transferable to your situation and pray it boldly. The fact that holy men have been this way before, gives you confidence to speak the same words into your circumstances. For instance, if God himself were to say to you through the greatest living prophet of your day, "You are going to die, you will not recover etc. etc," you actually have biblical precedent to not accept this verdict and plead for your life (2 Kings 20). Even Jesus, in the face of the most direct possible leading of God, that of his death on the cross, asked, "If it [is] possible, let this cup pass from me!" Too many of us passively accept every situation (most of which are not God's will), without even asking for a different verdict.

Other than the Psalms, the largest grouping of prayers that exist in the Bible, are the Prayers of the Prophets. Once you become familiar with all the prayers that have been included here, try to find more. Inherit their promises by faith. Look for an appropriate impassioned response to every facet of life. Then branch out and pray more of the prayers of the prophets yourself.

HEAR OH ISRAEL

Hear, O Israel:
The LORD our God, the LORD is one.
And you shall Love the LORD your God
with all your heart
and with all your soul
and with all your strength.

These commandments that I give you today
are to be upon your hearts.

Impress them on your children.
Talk about them when you sit at home
and when you walk along the road,
when you lie down and when you get up.
Tie them as symbols on your hands
and bind them on your foreheads.
Write them on the doorframes of your houses and on your gates.

When the LORD your God brings you into the land
He swore to your fathers, to Abraham, Isaac and Jacob,
to give you – a land with flourishing cities you did not build,
houses filled with all kinds of good things
you did not provide, wells you did not dig,
and vineyards and olive groves you did not plant—
then when you eat and are satisfied,
be careful that you do not forget the LORD,
who brought you out of Egypt, out of the land of slavery.

Deuteronomy 6:4 -12

MEDITATING ON THE LAW

Lord you have said . . .
"Be strong and very courageous."
So I ask for a strong and courageous heart.

Help me to be careful to obey all the law that Your
servant Moses gave us;
Give me the strength not turn from it
to the right or to the left
. . . so that I will be successful wherever I go.

And Father, today I declare,
I will not let this **Book of the Law** depart from my mouth;
but I will meditate on it day and night,
I will pray Your Law – the Bible,
out loud,
to you,
every day.
And as I pray Your word,
help me to be careful to do everything written in it.
Then I will prosper in everything I do . . .
and then I will have good success!

So as You have commanded me to be strong
and very courageous – I pray that I will be strong!
That I will not be terrified as I follow You;
that I will not be discouraged as I live out my faith,
for You Oh LORD are with me wherever I go."

Joshua 1:7-9*

THE PRAYER OF JABEZ
"OH THAT YOU WOULD BLESS ME"

Jabez was more honorable than his brothers.

His mother had named him Jabez,
Saying, "I gave birth to him in pain."

And Jabez called on the God of Israel saying,

"Oh, that You would bless me indeed,
and enlarge my territory,
that Your hand would be with me,
and that You would keep me from evil,
that I may not cause pain!"

So God granted him what he requested.

1 Chronicles 4:9-10 (NKJ)

FACE TO THE WALL - A PRAYER FOR HEALING

In those days Hezekiah became ill and was at the point of death. The prophet Isaiah son of Amoz went to him and said,

"This is what the LORD says:
Put your house in order, because you are going to die;
you will not recover."

Hezekiah turned his face to the wall and prayed to the LORD,
"Remember, O LORD,
how I have walked before you faithfully
and with wholehearted devotion
and have done what is good in Your eyes."

And Hezekiah wept bitterly.

I said, "In the prime of my life must I go through the gates of
death and be robbed of the rest of my years?"

I said, "I will not again see the LORD,
the LORD, in the land of the living;
no longer will I look on mankind,
or be with those who now dwell in this world.

Like a shepherd's tent my house has been pulled down
and taken from me.
Like a weaver I have rolled up my life,
and He has cut me off from the loom;
day and night You made an end of me.

I waited patiently till dawn,
but like a lion He broke all my bones;
day and night You made an end of me.

I cried like a crane or a swallow,
I moaned like a mourning dove.
My eyes grew weak as I looked to the heavens.
I am troubled; O Lord, come to my aid!"

Before Isaiah had left the middle court,
the word of the LORD came to him:
"Go back and tell Hezekiah, the leader of my people,
`This is what the LORD, the God of your father David, says:*

I have heard your prayer and seen your tears;
I will heal you.
On the third day from now
you will go up to the temple of the LORD.

I will add fifteen years to your life.
And I will deliver you and this family from this calamity

So Hezekiah praised the Lord and said,
What shall I say?
He has spoken to me, and He Himself has done this.
I will walk humbly all my years
because of this anguish of my soul.

Lord, by such things men live;
and my spirit finds life in them too.
You restored me to health and let me live.

Surely it was for my benefit that I suffered such anguish.
In Your love You kept me from the pit of destruction;
You have put all my sins behind your back.

For the grave cannot praise You,
death cannot sing Your praise;
those who go down to the pit cannot hope for Your faithfulness.

The living, the living-- they praise You, as I am doing today;
fathers tell their children about Your faithfulness.

The LORD will save me,
and we will sing with stringed instruments
all the days of our lives in the temple of the LORD.

Isaiah 38:1-3, 10-1; 2 Kings 20:4-6; 15-20; Isaiah 38: 15-20

JOB'S CONFESSION

**One day the angels came to present themselves before the
LORD, and Satan also came with them.**

The LORD said to Satan,
"Where have you come from?"
Satan answered the LORD,
"From roaming the earth and going back and forth in it."

Then the LORD said to Satan,
"Have you considered my servant Job?
There is no one on earth like him; he is blameless and upright,
a man who fears God and shuns evil."

"Does Job fear God for nothing?" Satan replied.
"Have you not put a hedge around him and his household
and everything he has? You have blessed the work of his hands,
so that his flocks and herds are spread throughout the land.
But stretch out your hand and strike everything he has,
and he will surely curse you to your face."

The LORD said to Satan,
"Very well, then, everything he has is in your hands,
but on the man himself do not lay a finger."
Then Satan went out from the presence of the LORD.

Then in one day Job's messengers came to him and said,
"your livestock has been stolen, your servants attacked,
and all your sons and daughters have been killed."

At this, Job got up and tore his robe and shaved his head.
Then he fell to the ground in worship and said:
"Naked I came from my mother's womb - naked I will depart.
The LORD gave
and the LORD has taken away;
blessed be the name of the LORD."

And Job prayed;
I know that my Redeemer lives,
and that in the end he will stand upon the earth.
And after my skin has been destroyed,
yet in my flesh I will see God;
I myself will see Him with my own eyes — I, and not another.
How my heart yearns within me!

And Job humbled himself before the Lord, and said;
"I know that You can do all things;
no plan of Yours can be thwarted.
You asked,
`Who is this that obscures My counsel without knowledge?*
'Surely I spoke of things I did not understand,
things too wonderful for me to know.
You said,
`Listen now, and I will speak;*
I will question you, and you shall answer Me.
Lord, 'My ears had heard of You
but now my eyes have seen You.
Therefore I despise myself and repent in dust and ashes."

*Job 1:6-12, 20; 19:25-27; 42:2-6 ***

OUR EYES ARE ON YOU

Some men came and told Jehoshaphat,
"A vast army is coming against you from Edom,
from the other side of the Sea.
It is already in En Gedi."

Alarmed, Jehoshaphat resolved to inquire of the LORD,
and he proclaimed a fast for all Judah.

The people of Judah came together
to seek help from the LORD;
indeed, they came from every town in Judah to seek Him.

Then Jehoshaphat stood up in the assembly of Judah
and Jerusalem at the temple of the LORD
in the front of the new courtyard and prayed:

"O LORD, God of our fathers,
are You not the God who is in heaven?
You rule over all the kingdoms of the nations.
Power and might are in Your hand,
and no one can withstand You.

O our God,
did you not drive out the inhabitants of this land
before Your people Israel
and give it forever to the descendants
of Abraham Your friend?
They have lived in it
and have built in it a sanctuary for Your Name, saying,

'If calamity comes upon us,
whether the sword of judgment, or plague or famine,
we will stand in Your presence
before this temple that bears Your Name
and will cry out to You in our distress,
and You will hear us and save us.'

"But now here are these men from a foreign land,
whose territory You would not allow Israel to invade
when they came from Egypt;
so they turned away from them and did not destroy them.

See how they are repaying us
by coming to drive us out of the possession
You gave us as an inheritance.

O our God, will You not judge them?
For we have no power to face this vast army that is attacking us.
We do not know what to do,
but our eyes are upon You."

Then the Spirit of the LORD came upon Jahaziel son of
Zechariah, this is what the LORD says to you:

'Do not be afraid or discouraged because of this vast army.
For the battle is not yours, but God's.
You will not have to fight this battle.
Take up your positions;
and stand firm and see the salvation of the LORD!"

2 Chronicles 20:2-12, 14a-15, 17*

THE VALLEY OF DRY BONES

The hand of the LORD was upon me,
and he brought me out by the Spirit of the LORD
and set me in the middle of a valley; it was full of bones.
He led me back and forth among them,
and I saw a great many bones on the floor of the valley,
bones that were very dry.

He asked me,
"Son of man, can these bones live?"

I said,
"O Sovereign LORD, You alone know."

Then he said to me,
"Prophesy to these bones and say to them,
'Dry bones, hear the word of the LORD!

This is what the Sovereign LORD says to these bones:
I will make breath enter you, and you will come to life.
I will attach tendons to you and make flesh come upon you
and cover you with skin;
I will put breath in you, and you will come to life.
Then you will know that I am the LORD.'"

So I prophesied as I was commanded.
And as I was prophesying, there was a noise, a rattling sound,
and the bones came together, bone to bone.
I looked, and tendons and flesh appeared on them
and skin covered them, but there was no breath in them.

Then he said to me,
"Prophesy to the breath;
prophesy, son of man, and say to it,

'This is what the Sovereign LORD says:
Come from the four winds, O breath,
and breathe into these slain, that they may live.'"

So I prophesied as He commanded me, and breath entered them;
they came to life and stood up on their feet – a vast army.

Then he said to me:
"Son of man, these bones are the whole house of Israel.
They say,
'Our bones are dried up and our hope is gone;
we are cut off.'

Therefore prophesy and say to them:
'This is what the Sovereign LORD says:
O my people, I am going to open your graves
and bring you up from them;
I will bring you back to the land of Israel.
Then you, My people, will know that I am the LORD,
when I open your graves and bring you up from them.
I will put My Spirit in you and you will live,
and I will settle you in your own land.

Then you will know that I the LORD have spoken,
and I have done it, declares the LORD.'"

Ezekiel 37:1-14

INTERCESSION FOR A NATION

In the first year of Darius son of Xerxes,
in the first year of his reign,
I, Daniel, understood from the Scriptures,
according to the word of the LORD
given to Jeremiah the prophet,
that the desolation of Jerusalem would last seventy years.

So I turned to the Lord God
and pleaded with Him in prayer and petition,
in fasting, and in sackcloth and ashes.

I prayed to the LORD my God and confessed:

***"O Lord, the great and awesome God,
who keeps His covenant of love with all who love Him
and obey His commands,
we have sinned and done wrong.
We have been wicked and have rebelled;
we have turned away from Your commands and laws.***

*We have not listened to Your servants the prophets,
who spoke in Your name to our kings,
our princes and our fathers,
and to all the people of the land.*

*"Lord, You are righteous,
but this day we are covered with shame—
we are covered with shame because we have sinned against You.*

All Israel has transgressed Your law and turned away,
refusing to obey You.
"Therefore the curses and sworn judgments
written in the Law of Moses,
the servant of God, have been poured out on us,
because we have sinned against You.

Under the whole heaven nothing has ever been done
like what has been done to Jerusalem.
The LORD did not hesitate to bring the disaster upon us,
for the LORD our God is righteous in everything He does;
yet we have not sought the favor of the LORD our God
by turning from our sins and giving attention to Your truth.

"Now, O Lord our God,
we have sinned . . . we have done wrong.
In keeping with all Your righteous acts,
turn away Your anger
and Your wrath from Jerusalem,
Your city, Your holy hill.

Our sins and the iniquities of our fathers
have made Jerusalem and Your people
an object of scorn to all those around us.

"Now, our God, hear the prayers and petitions of Your servant.
For Your sake, O Lord,
look with favor on Your desolate sanctuary.
Give ear, O God, and hear;
open Your eyes and see the desolation of the city
that bears Your Name.

We do not make requests of You because we are righteous, but because of Your great mercy.

O Lord, listen!
O Lord, forgive!
O Lord, hear and act!
For Your sake,
O my God, do not delay,
because your city
and Your people bear Your Name."

Daniel 9:1-8a, 11-19*

"THANK YOU GOD" - DAVIDS PRAYER

Then King David went in and sat before the LORD,
and he said:
"Who am I, O LORD God,
and what is my family,
that You have brought me this far?

And as if this were not enough in your sight, O God,
You have spoken about the future of the house of Your servant.
You have looked on me as though
I were the most exalted of men,
O LORD God.

"What more can I say to You for honoring Your servant?
For you know Your servant, O LORD.
For the sake of Your servant and according to your will,
You have done this great thing
and made known all these great promises.

"There is no one like You, O LORD,
and there is no God but You,
as we have heard with our own ears.

And who is like Your people Israel—
the one nation on earth
whose God went out to redeem a people for Himself,
and to make a name for Yourself,
and to perform great and awesome wonders
by driving out nations from before Your people,
whom You redeemed from Egypt?

You made Your people Israel Your very own forever,
and You, O LORD, have become their God.

"And now, LORD,
let the promise You have made
concerning Your servant and his house
be established forever.

Do as You promised,
so that it will be established
and that Your name will be great forever.
Then men will say, `The LORD Almighty,
the God over Israel, is Israel's God!'
And the house of Your servant David
will be established before You.

"You, my God, have revealed to Your servant
that You will build a house for him.
So your servant has found courage to pray to You.

O LORD, You are God!
You have promised these good things to Your servant.

Now You have been pleased to bless the house of Your servant,
that it may continue forever in Your sight;
for You, O LORD, have blessed it,
and it will be blessed forever."

1 Chronicles 17:16-27*

WHOLEHEARTED DEVOTION

David praised the LORD in the presence of the whole assembly,
saying, "Praise be to You, O LORD,
God of our father Israel, from everlasting to everlasting.

Yours, O LORD, is the greatness and the power
and the glory and the majesty and the splendor,
for everything in heaven and earth is Yours.
Yours, O LORD, is the kingdom;
You are exalted as head over all.

Wealth and honor come from You;
You are the ruler of all things.
In Your hands are strength and power
to exalt and give strength to all.

Now, our God, we give You thanks,
and praise Your glorious name.
"But who am I, and who are my people,
that we should be able to give as generously as this?
Everything comes from You,
and we have given You only what comes from Your hand.
We are aliens and strangers in Your sight,
as were all our forefathers.
Our days on earth are like a shadow, without hope.

O LORD our God, as for all this abundance
that we have provided for building You a temple
for Your Holy Name, it comes from Your hand,
and all of it belongs to You.

I know, my God, that You test the heart
and are pleased with integrity.

All these things have I given willingly and with honest intent.
And now I have seen with joy how willingly
Your people who are here have given to You.

O LORD, God of our fathers Abraham,
Isaac and Israel,
keep this desire in the hearts of Your people forever,
and keep their hearts loyal to You.

And give my sons and daughters
the wholehearted devotion to keep your commands,
requirements and decrees
and to do everything to build the kingdom
for which I have provided."

Then David said to the whole assembly,
"Praise the LORD your God."
So they all praised the LORD,
the God of their fathers;
they bowed low and fell prostrate
before the LORD and the king.

They ate and drank with great joy
in the presence of the LORD that day.

1 Chronicles 29:10-20, 22*

THE AARONIC BLESSING

The LORD said to Moses,

"Tell Aaron and his sons,
`This is how you are to bless the Israelites.
Say to them:
The LORD bless you . . . and keep you;
the LORD make his face shine upon you
. . . and be gracious to you;
the LORD turn his face toward you
. . . and give you peace.

So they will put My name on the Israelites,
and I will bless them."

Numbers 6:22-27

THE PRAYERS OF JESUS

Heaven and earth will pass away,
but my words will never pass away.

INTRODUCTION TO PRAYING THE PRAYERS OF JESUS

Every prayer of Jesus should become the prayer of every Christian. By praying the prayers of Jesus, one is engaging in the highest form of discipleship. "It is enough for the . . . servant [to be] like his Master" (Matt. 10:25). It is not only that Jesus prayed more than anyone else, but also the content of his prayers differed from every other persons' prayers in the Bible. Although fully human, from childhood onwards, he had a knowledge of both the words and the intent of Scripture. Thus, when in the Temple at the tender age of twelve, he was able to dialogue with his teachers to such an extent that, "everyone who heard him was amazed at his understanding and his answers" (Luke 2:47). As Jesus grew, he would go to solitary places to pray (Mark 1:35). He prayed with such intensity that it came with "loud cries and tears" (Hebrews 5:7), and so earnestly that his "sweat was like drops of blood falling to the ground" (Luke 22:44). The whole lifestyle of prayer that Jesus models for us has scarcely been touched by most Christians. But, when the prayers of Jesus are prayed back to Him, one will slowly come to realize what Jesus so obviously knew about prayer. His words will lead you into his prayer experience, and then . . . into the fellowship of sonship that he himself enjoyed with his Father.

You see, Jesus modeled a relationship with YAHWEH that was radical for his day. Up to that point, no one in history had ever addressed the Lord God Almighty in the way Jesus did. Devout Jews were afraid of even using God's name - *YaHWeH* - for fear of taking His name in vain. In order to avoid this, elaborate systems had been set up so that Jews could refer to *Yahweh* without actually saying His name. Rather than pronounce the sacred name, Jews would say "my Lord" (*Adonai*). Even as late as the medieval period, the vowels of Adonai were attached to the consonants YHWH, resulting in the word *Jehovah*.[1] Therefore, it was quite a shock for Jesus to come from the entirely opposite end of the spectrum and address God as '*abba pater*' or 'dear Daddy' (Mk. 14:36). This term of endearment was nothing less than revolutionary. Even slaves could not address the head of the house as '*abba*', because it was thought to be too personal. Normally only infants and children used this innocent, common word for their own "Daddies". But, never would a Jew address God in such terms. So, Jesus was opening the door to an entirely new degree of intimacy when he instructed his disciples to pray "Our *Father*, who is in heaven . . ." (Mt. 6:9). In this way, he introduces us to a new relationship with God - one that resembles the intimacy and familiarity of a 'daddy' with his child.

Jesus' prayers are also unique in that he is still praying them today. The writer to the Hebrews encourages us by saying that, "because Jesus lives forever, he has a permanent priesthood. Therefore he is able to save completely those who come to God through him, because he always lives to intercede for them" (Heb. 7:24-25). In a very real sense, he is even praying for you right now. Jesus' prayer for Peter, therefore, becomes an example of what he is praying for us now. At that time, Jesus said to Peter: "Simon, Simon, Satan has *asked* (demanded for trial) to sift *you* (plural) as wheat. But I have prayed for *you* (singular), Simon, that your faith may not fail (Luke 22:31-32a)." Jesus was not saying that only Peter was being set up for severe trail and testing. No, he was indicating that all twelve of them would be tested and tried, and that He was praying for all twelve of them. But he prayed for Peter, in particular. "I have prayed for *you* (singular), and when you have turned back, strengthen your brothers." Because Jesus still lives and intercedes for us, this prayer can be extended to all of us who, in similar ways, are singled out for trial and testing. Who amongst us does not need Jesus' ongoing, continual intercession? Practically speaking, we could put our own names into Jesus' prayers (cf. Matt. 6:13), or pray them for our own disciples. Therefore, when you pray the prayers of Jesus, you are joining with him in his heavenly intercession. In this way, Jesus' prayers are as relevant today as when they were first prayed.

Yet there are even more ways to approach these prayers. As we begin to pray the prayers of Jesus, we start by praying the text at face value, agreeing with Jesus in the historical and theological context of the people and things that he prayed for. When he prays for his disciples, petitioning God for this or that, you, too, could embrace the historical context of these prayers. You may start your own prayers by simply being reminded of the twelve who were with him at his passion, and the church that grew out of their testimony. When you pray the prayer of Jesus: "Glorify your Son, that your Son may glorify you," you are agreeing with Jesus and continuing to pray for the glory of the Son to be manifest. This might be a simple prayer of agreement, where we also long for Jesus to be glorified today, and that his life and passion will continue to bring glory to the Father now. In this way we are praying today for the same things Jesus prayed for then.

At a deeper level, as the intercessor continues to pray the prayers over and over again, saying the same words that Jesus said, it becomes apparent how Jesus thought. What was Jesus asking for? What were his concerns? By praying his words, we enter his mind and spirit – his passion. Soon his concerns become our concerns and his words our words. As this happens, we can then begin to apply the same prayers to similar contexts in our own lives. We can also ask God to be glorified in *our* lives by what *we* do. We can ask for his will to be done in our choices. We can pray for our own families, friends, and loved ones in the same way that Jesus prayed for his disciples. His concerns for his disciples were for protection and unity (John 17:11-12), for joy in the midst of a hostile world (John 17:13-16), and for practical holiness grown by the word of truth (John 17:17-19). It is a small step for any committed Christian to turn these classic texts into primary concerns for his/her own disciples. Again, we see the application of Jesus' prayers to our own personal contexts.

Further, by praying the prayers of Jesus, as though they were our own prayers, we become types of Christ *(anointed ones),* asking these things of God for ourselves. As mentioned earlier, Jesus enjoyed a special place as the Son of God and, as such, talked to God with a boldness unknown to others. John 17 is loaded with things the average Christian would never dare utter. But as we pray the words, slowly it begins to dawn on us that "as You [the Father] sent Me [the Son] into the world, I [Jesus] have sent them [all Christians] into the world (17:18)." We see that the things that Jesus did, we are to do because Jesus has given us the same glory that the Father gave him (17:22).

Therefore, we, too, should be glorifying the Father with our lives just as Jesus did with his (17:1). Since the Father granted Christ all authority over all people, by extension, Jesus was is also able to give his followers all authority to go in his name as dispensers of eternal life (Matt. 28:18). Praying Jesus' prayers imbues our spirits with the understanding that the whole of our lives is to be patterned after the whole of his. We see that we also have a work to accomplish as we move towards our own passion when we, too, will be raised incorruptible with a glorious body. The Father will glorify us as we go to be with him (1 Cor. 15:40-42). Paul even prays that we would know with an intimate knowing. . . the hope, the inheritance, and the incomparably great power for us who believe. That power is like the working of his mighty strength, which he exerted in Christ when he raised him from the dead and seated him at his right hand in the heavenly realms (Eph 1:19-20).

This is huge! The power that raised Jesus from the dead and brought glory to the Father is the same power that is in us now while we are alive! Praying the Prayers of Jesus leads us to the place where Jesus *was* – and where he intends us *to go*.

The eventuality that results from praying Jesus' prayers is that we find ourselves tracing our lives after his. Peter said, "To this you were called, because Christ suffered for you, leaving you an *example*, that you should follow in his steps (1 Pet 2:21)." The word *example* is from the Greek compound word *hupo* (under) and *grammos* (writing) – literally, an 'under-writing.' In a real sense, the life of Jesus is the prototype or pattern, the real representation that all Christians use as the master copy from which to trace our lives. We are imitators of Him. And nothing accomplishes this in our toddler stages like saying his prayers with our names in them. By filling our hearts and mouths with the very words of Jesus, his essence is formed in us. We begin to believe that we really are Christians – "little Christ ones" – meant to live the same supernatural, miraculous life of love that Jesus did.

Lastly, we have included the "Jesus Prayer." This prayer grew out of the desire to follow the biblical injunction to "pray without ceasing." It has been given different names at different times in church history, such as "breath prayer," "centering prayer," "monastic prayer," and "contemplative prayer." Although there are differing nuances with each of the labels, the essence of this style of prayer is the same. It is an extremely simple and pure form, which has as its goal to be constantly in the presence of God. This method can be used by anyone, because it is not a prayer that is based on intellect, but on experience. Moses once prayed, "If your presence does not go with us, then do not lead us up from here." In one sentence, Moses captures the longing of the "Jesus Prayer". Its desire is to constantly remain in the felt presence of God. This lofty goal of perpetual prayer is achieved by a very simple means. The prayer itself can not be more uncomplicated. As the author of *The Cloud of Unknowing* says, "A one-syllable word such as 'God' or 'love' is best." Through repeating a word or phrase over and over again, until it becomes to us as natural as breathing, our spirits become so immersed in communion with God, that we are able to "live in the shadow of the Almighty," to "abide in the vine," to "pray without ceasing." This method of prayer originated from the time of the Desert Fathers, and was later incorporated into the Greek Orthodox tradition. The simple three or four phrases they chose to pray came out of a parable Jesus told in Luke 18:13. It was later changed to address the Lord Jesus, and thus the title the "Jesus Prayer." The prayer is as follows: *'Jesus Christ, Son of*

God, have mercy on me, a sinner.' Nuances may change, in that you may make it *Lord Jesus Christ*, or you may drop the phrase, *a sinner*. But in the end it is a simple phrase or thought, the size of a breath, that requires focus which directs the mind, in order to affect the heart, ultimately moving the spirit. An excellent illustration of this is found in *The Way of a Pilgrim*, a beautiful story of a Russian peasant seeking the answer to unceasing prayer. After his mentor told him to pray the "Jesus Prayer" up to twelve thousand times a day he eventually mastered it until he was swept away in God's presence. He describes his experience by saying:

". . . that after receiving this direction, I spent the rest of the summer reciting the name of Jesus vocally and I enjoyed great peace. During my sleep I often dreamed that I was praying. And if I happened to meet people in the day they all seemed to me to be kinsmen, even though I did not know them. My thoughts had quieted down completely; I thought only of the Prayer to which my heart began to listen, and my heart produced certain warmth and gladness . . . . My solitary hut was to me like a splendid palace, and I did not know how to thank God for sending me, a great sinner, such a holy elder for a director. So now I walk and say the Jesus Prayer without ceasing, and it is more precious and sweet to me than anything else in the world . . . . I walk in a semi-conscious state without worries, interest, and temptations. My only desire and attraction is for solitude and ceaseless recitation of the Jesus Prayer. This makes me happy. God knows what this is all about."[1]

Thus, whether we are moving toward the experience of continual communion with God by praying the "Jesus Prayer," or whether we are entering the mind of Christ through the longer, didactic Prayers of Jesus, we are to follow Jesus in his prayer example. He taught us by word and deed how to pray. Therefore, 'every prayer of Jesus should become the prayer of every Christian.'

THE LORD'S PRAYER

"This, then, is how you should pray:

***"Our Father . . . who is in heaven,
holy is Your name,***

*let Your kingdom come,
let Your will be done
on earth . . . as it is in heaven.*

Give us today our daily bread.

Forgive us our sins,
as we forgive those who sin against us.

And do not let us be lead us not into temptation,
but deliver us from the evil one.

***For Yours is the kingdom
and the power,
and the glory,
for ever and ever . . .***

Amen, and AMEN!

Matthew 6:9 – 13; NIV & NKJV *

GLORIFY YOUR NAME

Now my heart is troubled,
and what shall I say?

`Father, save me from this hour'?*

No, it was for this very reason
I came to this hour.

"Father, glorify Your name!"

Then a voice came from heaven,
*"I have glorified it,
and will glorify it again."*

John 12:27-28

GLORIFY YOUR SON

After Jesus said this, he looked toward heaven and prayed:

"Father, the time has come.
Glorify Your Son,
that Your Son may glorify You.

For You granted him authority over all people
that he might give eternal life
to all those You have given him.

Now this is eternal life:
that they may know You,
the only true God,
and Jesus Christ,
whom You have sent.

I have brought You glory
on earth by completing the work
You gave me to do.

And now, Father,
glorify me in Your presence
with the glory I had with You
before the world began.

John 17:1-5

A PRAYER FOR DISCIPLES

"Father, I have revealed You to those
whom You gave me out of the world.

They were Yours;
You gave them to me and they have obeyed Your word.
Now they know that everything You have given me
comes from You.
For I gave them the words You gave me
and they accepted them.
They knew with certainty that I came from You,
and they believed that You sent me.

I pray for them.
I am not praying for the world,
but for those You have given me,
for they are Yours.

All I have is Yours,
and all You have is mine.
And glory has come to me through them.

I will remain in the world no longer,
but they are still in the world,
and I am coming to You.

Holy Father,
protect them by the power of Your name –
the name You gave me –
so that they may be one as we are one.

While I was with them,
I protected them and kept them safe by that name You gave me.
None has been lost except the one doomed to destruction
so that Scripture would be fulfilled.

I am coming to You now,
but I say these things while I am still in the world,
so that they may have the full measure of my joy –
the joy of Jesus – within them.

I have given them Your word
and the world has hated them,
for they are not of the world
any more than I am of the world.

My prayer is not that You take them out of the world
but that You protect them from the evil one.
They are not of the world, even as I am not of it.

Sanctify them by the truth . . . Your word is truth.

As You sent me into the world,
I have sent them into the world.

For their sakes I sanctify myself,
that they too may be sanctified
through the truth.

John 17:6-19*

UNTO UNITY, GLORY, AND LOVE

"My prayer is not for them alone.
I pray also for those who will believe in me
through their message,
that all of them may be one,
just as You Father, are in me and I am in You.

May they also be in us
so that the world may believe that You have sent me.
I have given them the glory that You gave me,
that they may be one ... as we are one:
I in them and You in me.
May they be brought to complete unity
to let the world know that You sent me
and have loved them even as You have loved me.

"Father, I want those You have given me
to be with me where I am, and to see my glory,
the glory You have given me
because You loved me before the creation of the world.

"Righteous Father,
though the world does not know You, I know You,
and they know that You have sent me.
I have made You known to them,
and will continue to make You known
in order that the love You have for me may be in them
and that I myself may be in them."*

John 17:20-26

WHEN YOU ARE CONVERTED

Simon, Simon,
Satan has asked to sift you as wheat.

But I have prayed for you,
Simon,
that your faith may not fail.

And when you are converted,
and have turned back,
strengthen your brothers.

Luke 22:31-32

YOUR WILL BE DONE

Going a little farther,
he fell with his face to the ground and prayed,

"My Father,
if it is possible,
take this cup away from me;
nevertheless not My will,
but Yours, be done."

Then he returned to his disciples
and found them sleeping.
"Could you men not keep watch
with me for one hour?"

"Watch and pray
so that you will not fall into temptation.
The spirit is willing,
but the body is weak."

He went away a second time
and being in anguish, he prayed more earnestly,
and his sweat was like drops of blood falling to the ground.

"My Father,
if it is not possible for this cup to be taken away
. . . unless I drink it,
let Your will be done."

Matthew 26:39 – 42; Luke 22:42, 44*

FATHER FORGIVE THEM

When they came to the place called the Skull,
there they crucified him,
along with the criminals —
one on his right,
the other on his left.

And Jesus said,
*"Father, forgive them,
for they do not know what they are doing."*

And they divided up his clothes by casting lots.

About the ninth hour Jesus cried out in a loud voice,
"Eloi, Eloi, lama sabachthani?"
– which means,
"My God, my God, why have you forsaken me?"

Then Jesus called out with a loud voice,
"Father, into Your hands I commit my spirit."

When he had said this, he breathed his last.

Matthew 27:45-46; Luke 23:33-34, 46

THE JESUS PRAYER

"Lord Jesus Christ,

Son of God,

have mercy on me,

a sinner."

The Philokalia

APOSTOLIC PRAYERS

I urge, then, first of all,
that requests, prayers, intercession
and thanksgiving be made for everyone

INTRODUCTION TO PRAYING THE APOSTOLIC PRAYERS

Have you ever listened to a father earnestly pray for his child? In the Apostolic Prayers, you find the apostles – the early fathers of the church – praying for their spiritual children. Most of the Apostolic Prayers in the Bible were written by the Apostle Paul. And Paul was, as he put it, a father. "Even though you have ten thousand guardians in Christ, you do not have many fathers, for in Christ Jesus I became your father through the gospel" (1 Cor. 4:15). Therefore, in these prayers you hear a father praying – which is a different form of prayer than is found anywhere else in the Bible.

As one of the most pharisaical Jews in history, Paul was eminently endowed with the credentials to create a new prayer genre. His life had been devoted to 'meditating on the law day and night.' He would have known the Psalms almost by heart. He studied the Torah and the traditions so intricately that he burned with murderous zeal against those who opposed them. Then, he had the cataclysmic, personal revelation of *Messiah*, complete with the proverbial 'knocked off his horse' experience. This 'new' revelation did not detract from his lifelong learning - it only added to it! Moreover, Paul received numerous visions and revelations directly from the Spirit of God. Therefore, when Paul prays, he prays as one rooted and grounded in the historical 'faith of his fathers,' yet with the full understanding of *Messiah* that all of the prophets had been waiting for.

As Abraham was the father of all who believe, so Paul, Peter and John became fathers of the fullness of the apostolic faith. Hence, the Apostolic Prayers are fatherly prayers. They express what a father wants for those he has birthed and is raising in the Lord. They are filled with love, longing, and wisdom. Peppered with words of affection, the tone of these prayers is often pastoral and tender. These fathers condense lessons learned from a life of following Jesus, and intercede specifically for the things that they know will be the most difficult, or most necessary, for their sons and daughters in a given region. If parents today were to stop and write down the best of their desires for their own children, they would find expression in the apostolic prayers. Only, the Apostolic Prayers would express these desires far better than any parent ever could because they were originally inspired from the heart of *the* Father – God.

The Apostolic Prayers are also foundational prayers. As founders of the church, the apostles were setting things in order. They were grounding the disciples of Jesus into the essential theological basics that a child of God would need to grow in his/her life in the Spirit. Therefore, they include necessary truths, not flowery extras. They focus on character, on the knowledge of God, and on the power of the Spirit-filled life. Because of this, they are easily transferable to our lives today. For example, many people pray to know God's will in their lives. They ask whether they should take this job or that job; or whether they should go here or go there? Yet when one prays the Apostolic Prayers, the emphasis is different. In the Bible, being filled with the knowledge of God's will includes such things as "bearing fruit in every good work and growing in the knowledge of God" (Col. 1:10). The will of God, in the biblical sense, is not so much about going to this location or that location, but rather about bearing fruit *while* we are going. The emphasis on doing the will of God in the Apostolic Prayers is that, wherever we end up and whatever we do, are we actually getting to know God better? If not, then we are probably out of his will. Further, the understanding of "bearing fruit" includes good works, discipleship, and character issues. By consistently praying the concerns of the Apostolic Prayers, we will sort out so much of the chatter and misapplication of our contemporary, biblically illiterate prayers.

The Apostolic Prayers have several features that are worth noting. A primary consideration is that they are *God-focused*. They are, in fact, so God-focused that they virtually ignore the demonic hosts. The Apostolic Prayers never address Satan, either to rebuke him or bind him. When the apostles prayed, they prayed directly to the Father and asked him to deal with any obstacles that may be standing in the way of their prayers. They directed their appeals to the Father, in the name of the Son, for answers generated by the power of the Holy Spirit. This does not mean that we cannot follow Jesus' or Paul's example of rebuking sin, sickness and demonic spirits. As Mike Bickle says,

> *The Holy Spirit on specific occasions may lead the church to war against a principality. I see this a governmental function requiring unity among those in spiritual authority. Such strategic warfare is Divinely orchestrated by the Holy Spirit on prophetic occasions.* [1]

There are times when such prayers are needed. However, this is different than what is found in the Apostolic Prayers. In the case of New Testament prayers, the predominant pattern is to pray to the Father. We appeal to him to see things accomplished in the church, thus opening the way for the Holy Spirit to convict the world of sin, righteousness, and judgment.

In addition to a God-ward focus, apostolic prayers are *positive* prayers. They ask that we would be filled with good things, that we would prosper, that we would increase in the knowledge of God. Apostolic Prayers are not focused on fixing what we aren't, but rather on fulfilling what we can be. Rather than telling God how bad everything is and how rotten the world is getting, for example, these prayers ask for joy to increase, and grace to abound. Rather than preaching prayers that tell everyone else what they ought to do, Apostolic Prayers speak directly to God, and asked him to accomplish his desired goals. They petition him for people to be filled with the Holy Spirit, and for the church to flourish through the manifestation of the gifts and fruit of the Spirit (i.e. the preaching of the word, prophetic revelation, signs and wonders, love, unity, etc.). And such positive prayers beget positive results.

Finally, Apostolic Prayers are mostly *for the Church*. They bring before God the concerns of the saved, whether individuals, churches, or regions. This means that Apostolic Prayers are meant to be prayed with someone, or someplace, specifically in mind. These are not "God bless the whole wide world" prayers! When praying these prayers for yourself, personalize them by changing the pronouns and ask that God would do these things in your own life. Then, pray the exact same words over your friends and family, putting their names into the text. Do the same for your church and the other churches throughout your city or region. When you do this, you will be praying like the apostles prayed. You can even expect the same results!

Since they are for the Church, Apostolic Prayers are almost exclusively for the saved. This is a significant point, considering how many intercessors only want to pray for the lost and, in so doing, disregard the church. There is a dangerous tendency for intercessors is to become discouraged and angry with the Church, and to begin to concentrate their great prayer burden almost exclusively on the lost. But Apostolic Prayers focus on the Church, to the end that Christians become filled with the power and gifts of God so that they – as empowered ones - will reach the lost. This is how Jesus, himself, taught us to pray. He said, "The harvest is plentiful but the workers are few. *Ask the Lord of the harvest, therefore, to send out workers* into his harvest field (Matt. 9:37-38)." While we are called to love our neighbor, Apostolic Prayers ensure that we don't neglect our spiritual family.

All that remains, then, is to pray the Apostolic Prayers. Although this sounds easy enough, a person will not be long in praying them before he/she discovers that every word is packed with meaning. We suggest that you pray them slowly, phrase by phrase, or even word by word, until you know exactly the meaning and intent of each word. Stop and ruminate on the depth of what is being asked for – and keep a commentary handy for those easily misunderstood theological concepts. As Peter said, "[Paul's] letters contain some things that are hard to understand . . . (2 Peter 3:15-16)". As with all prayer, you cannot pray well when you don't know what you are asking for. So take your time. Pray slowly. Look up words and concepts you don't understand. And, above all else, ask the Father to give you, through these prayers, a revelation of his heart.

REVIVAL POWER

When they heard this,
they raised their voices together in prayer to God.
"Sovereign Lord," they said,
"You made the heaven and the earth and the sea,
and everything in them.
You spoke by the Holy Spirit
through the mouth of Your servant, our father David:

'Why do the nations rage and the peoples plot in vain?
The kings of the earth take their stand
and the rulers gather together
against the Lord and against His Anointed One.'

Indeed they have conspired against Your holy servant Jesus,
whom You anointed.
They did what Your power and will
had decided beforehand should happen.

Now, Lord, consider their threats
and enable Your servants to speak Your word with great boldness.
Stretch out Your hand to heal
and perform miraculous signs and wonders
through the name of Your holy servant Jesus."

After they prayed, the place where they were meeting was shaken.
And they were all filled with the Holy Spirit
and spoke the word of God boldly.

Acts 4:29-31

REVIVAL OF DIVINE REVELATION

For this reason,
ever since I heard about your faith
in the Lord Jesus
and your love for all the saints,

I have not stopped giving thanks for you,
remembering you in my prayers.

I keep asking that the God of our Lord Jesus Christ,
the glorious Father,
may give you the Spirit of wisdom and revelation,
so that you may know him better.

I pray also
that the eyes of your heart may be enlightened
in order that
you may know the hope to which He has called you,
the riches of His glorious inheritance in the saints,
and His incomparably great power for us who believe.

That power is like the working of His mighty strength,
which He exerted in Christ
when He raised Him from the dead
and seated Him at His right hand
in the heavenly realms,

Ephesians 1:15-20

THE OUTPOURING OF DIVINE LOVE

For this reason I kneel before the Father,
from whom His whole family in heaven
and on earth derives its name.

I pray that out of his glorious riches
He may strengthen you with power
through his Spirit in your inner being,
so that Christ may dwell in your hearts through faith.
And I pray that you,
being rooted and established in love,
may have power, together with all the saints,
to grasp how wide
and long
and high
and deep
is the love of Christ,
and to know this love that surpasses knowledge—
that you may be filled to the measure
of all the fullness of God.

Now to Him who is able to do immeasurably more
than all we ask or imagine,
according to His power that is at work within us,
to Him be glory in the church and in Christ Jesus
throughout all generations,
for ever and ever!
Amen.

Ephesians 3:14-21

THE RELEASE OF PROPHETIC BOLDNESS

And pray in the Spirit
with all kinds of prayers
and requests.

*With this in mind,
be alert and always keep on praying
for all the saints.*

**Pray also for me,
that whenever I open my mouth,
words may be given me
so that I will fearlessly
make known the mystery of the gospel,
for which I am an ambassador in chains.**

**Pray that I may declare it fearlessly,
as I should.**

Ephesians 6:18-20

OVERFLOWING HOLY LOVE

I thank my God every time I remember you.

In all my prayers for all of you,
I always pray with joy

And this is my prayer:
that your love may abound
more and more
in knowledge and depth of insight,
so that
you may be able to discern
what is best
and may be pure
and blameless
until the day of Christ,

filled with the fruit of righteousness
that comes through Jesus Christ—
to the glory and praise of God.

Philippians 1:3-4, 9-11

FILLED WITH A KNOWLEDGE OF HIS WILL

To the holy and faithful brothers in Christ:
Grace and peace to you from God our Father.
We always thank God, the Father of our Lord Jesus Christ,
when we pray for you,
because we have heard of your faith in Christ Jesus
and of the love you have for all the saints.

For this reason, since the day we heard about you,
we have not stopped praying for you,
asking God to fill you with the knowledge of His will
through all spiritual wisdom and understanding.

And we pray this in order that
you may live a life worthy of the Lord
and may please Him in every way:
bearing fruit in every good work,
growing in the knowledge of God,

being strengthened with all power
according to His glorious might
so that you may have great endurance
and patience,
and joyfully give thanks to the Father . . .

Who has qualified you to share in the
inheritance of the saints in the kingdom of light.

Colossians 1:2 – 4, 9-12

THE DOOR OF GOD

Devote yourselves to prayer,
being watchful and thankful.

And pray for us, too,
that
God may open a door
for our message,
so that we may proclaim
the mystery of Christ,
for which I am in chains.

Pray that I may proclaim it clearly,
as I should.

Also, I,
who am one of you and a servant of Christ Jesus,
send you greetings.

I am always wrestling in prayer for you,
that you may stand firm in all the will of God,
mature and fully assured.

Colossians 4:3-4, 12

THE ESTABLISHED HEART

How can we thank God enough for you
in return for all the joy we have
in the presence of our God because of you?
Night and day we pray most earnestly
that we may see you again
and supply what is lacking in your faith.

Now may our God and Father Himself
and our Lord Jesus clear the way for us to come to you.

May the Lord
make your love increase and overflow for each other
and for everyone else, just as ours does for you.

May He strengthen and establish your hearts
so that you will be blameless and holy
in the presence of our God and Father
when our Lord Jesus comes with all His holy ones.

May God himself, the God of peace,
sanctify you through and through.
May your whole spirit, soul and body
be kept blameless at the coming of our Lord Jesus Christ.

The One who calls you is faithful
and He will do it.
Brothers, pray for us.

1 Thessalonians 3:9-13; 5: 23-25

FULFILL YOUR CALL

We ought always to thank God for you, brothers, and rightly so,
because your faith is growing more and more,
and the love every one of you has for each
other is increasing.

With this in mind,
we constantly pray for you,
***that our God may count you worthy of His calling,
and that by His power
He may fulfill every good purpose of yours
and every act prompted by your faith.***

***We pray this so that the name of our Lord Jesus
may be glorified in you,
and you in Him,
according to the grace of our God
and the Lord Jesus Christ.***

2 Thessalonians 1:3, 11-12

INCREASE YOUR WORD

Finally, brothers,
pray for us that the message of the Lord
may spread rapidly
and be honored,
just as it was with you.

And pray that we may be delivered
from wicked and evil men,
for not everyone has faith.

But the Lord is faithful,
and He will strengthen
and protect you from the evil one.

May the Lord direct your hearts into God's love
and Christ's perseverance.

Now may the Lord of peace Himself give you peace
at all times and in every way.

The Lord be with all of you.

2 Thessalonians 3:1-3, 5, 16

JUST SAY NO!

For the grace of God that brings salvation
has appeared to all men.

It teaches us to say
"No"
to ungodliness
and worldly passions,

and to live self-controlled,
upright
and godly lives
in this present age,

while we wait for the blessed hope—
the glorious appearing
of our great God
and Savior, Jesus Christ,

Titus 2:11-13

A PRAYER OF PROSPERITY

Dear friend,
I pray that you may enjoy good health

and that in all respects,
everything may go well with you,
even as your soul is getting along well.

That you may prosper in all things,
just as your soul prospers.

3 John 2

JUDE'S DOXOLOGY

Now unto Him
who is able to keep you from falling
and to present you standing
before His glorious presence
without fault and with great joy—

to the only God our Savior
be glory,
majesty,
power
and authority,

through Jesus Christ our Lord,
before all ages,
now and forevermore!

Amen.

Jude 1: 24-25

THE APOSTOLIC BENEDICTION

Finally, brothers
. . . goodbye.

Aim for perfection,
listen to my appeal,
be of one mind,
live in peace.

And the God of love and peace
will be with you.

Greet one another with a holy kiss.

All the saints send their greetings.

May the grace of the Lord Jesus Christ,
and the love of God,
and the fellowship of the Holy Spirit
be with you all.

Amen & Amen!

2 Corinthians 13:11-14

HYMNS OF THE REVELATION

Blessed is the one who reads the words of this prophecy, and blessed are those who hear it and take to heart what is written in it, because the time is near.

INTRODUCTION TO PRAYING THE HYMNS OF THE REVELATION

In life, when you don't know the outcome of a given trial, you may be tempted to quit in the middle. That is why the 'Book of the Revelation of Jesus Christ' – in which Jesus is 'revealed' as the totally triumphant, conquering King of Kings – must become an integral part of the prayer life of every believer. John begins the book saying, "blessed is the one who reads and hears the words of this prophecy" (1:3). Having had a series of visions of what lay ahead for the Church, he knew what was coming. He knew the future would not be easy, but he also knew the final outcome. He echoes the last sentiments of Jesus to the apostles: "In this world you will have tribulation – but take heart, I have overcome the world" (John 16:33). Praying the Hymns of the Revelation will give faith to every suffering Christian, perspective to every unjust situation, and hope to every one who feels like giving up. Weak people will be transformed into overcomers, because the praying the hymns shows us what is going on in the eternal world while we live life in the temporal one. In the book of Revelation, we have gone 'back to the future,' and thus our vantage point of the present is different. Regardless of one's theological interpretation of the book, all things ultimately conclude with the bodily return of Jesus Christ, and a new heaven and new earth (19 – 22). To that end, we pray these prayers with a future, forwarding-looking emphasis. No matter what your state on earth now, things are going to get better. We have a real future and a real hope.

A distinct feature of the hymns of the Revelation is that they reveal the attitude of heaven about the judgments of God on earth. Heaven is not neutral to these judgments. In fact, there is vigorous agreement by all the created order, that justice has come at last. The martyrs cry out, "How long oh God, until you avenge our blood?" (6:10) The angel with the bowl of wrath says, "They poured out the blood of saints and prophets, and you have given them blood to drink. They deserve it." To which the altar responds, "Just and true, are your judgments. . ." (16:5-7 NASB). The elders declare, "The time has come for judging the dead . . . and for destroying those who destroy the earth" (11:18). These are not the types of prayers that most of us would normally say. But heaven says them and, therefore, we must say them too. Regularly praying heaven's prayers aligns us with heaven's perspective. Finally, God is making all wrongs right. Finally, he is bringing an end to sin and sorrow. Finally, he wins the war. In the word of the living creatures, "Amen!"

Therefore, heaven is not sad. Heaven is jubilant, victorious, and exultant – which is why the hymns must be prayed *out loud* and *loud*. Repeatedly throughout the book, John says that every being in heaven is shouting or singing in "a LOUD voice." He shows us that heavenly worship is not only *out loud* – it is also *loud*! Over twenty-two times, John notes that the praise, prayers, and declarations of the angels in heaven are loud. In heaven, speech is described as being like the roar of a lion, the sound of an ocean, or a sound like thunder. The seven thunders of judgment are said to "utter their voice" (10:3). Why is everything loud? What is the reason for the volume? Why do people and angels and living creatures sing, shout, praise, declare, etc . . . so loudly?

Simply stated, the reason is passion! Passion is at the root of *out loud* and *loud*. Because of fear, a timid mother will cry out. Anger will make a parent shout. Excitement will cause a crowd to roar; victory, an army to shout; affirmation, a fan to cheer; and joy, a group to yell. Behind each of these emotions is passion and passion incites *loud*. Conversely, if someone is bored, depressed, or passionless, they are not loud. It takes focus and energy to have volume in your voice. It's hard to be loud if you are not into it, because loud takes effort. What is it that those in heaven see that gives them so much inspiration? Obviously, there is something to the unobstructed, face-to-face encounter with God that blows away any bored lackadaisical attitudes. Does it say something about our knowledge of God when we will not lift up our voice on earth? Simply put, our own inability to pray *out loud* and *loud* exposes a deficiency of passion, because loud is part of what is meant by loving God with all our *soul* and *strength*.

Many people, particularly in the Western world, have a distinct aversion to praying *out loud* and *loud*. Why? Most likely because they do not know what to say and they are not really into it. They pray silent prayers in their minds by default. Even if people do have the words – in the form of a psalm, a hymn, or a prayer – their prayers often feel flat and lifeless. However, just the very doing of it, and doing it *loud,* can affect your passion and *vice versa*. Sometimes going for it verbally increases passion. Even when you may not feel into it, as you discipline your soul to "stand up and praise the Lord" (Neh. 9:5), zeal and encouragement will invariably take over.

This principle is true in our daily lives. People just have to talk about certain subjects and passionate feelings are evoked. So, when it comes to the issue of prayer, the question could be asked: "Do you pray out loud to God because you are into it? Or do you pray out loud by faith, feeling nothing, and trust that God is hearing and will answer?" Of course, the answer is both. We come to God by faith and the practical bonus of praying *out loud* and *loud* is that, eventually, we ourselves are impacted by what we are saying. Eventually, our emotions will be affected if we discipline our wills to give a *sacrifice of praise*. All too often we are led by the impulses of the moment. If we don't feel excited, passionate, or zealous in spirit at that moment, we do not stir ourselves to actually give the *sacrifice* of praise. However, when it comes to prayer, we do not have to passively wait for the waters to be stirred – we can stir them ourselves just by praying *out loud* and *loud*!

This is especially true when praying the Hymns of the Revelation because the words of these hymns are packed with emotion. As you pray them, you will discover that there are at least ten worship words. The worship words are short, strong words such as power, wealth, wisdom, strength, honor, glory, praise, blessing, might, and dominion (5:12, 7:12, 1:6). There are also five victory chants: 'Worthy is the Lamb' (5:12), 'Salvation to our God' (7:10), 'Holy, Holy, Holy' (4:8), 'Great and marvelous', and 'Just and true' (15:3)'. In addition to these, there are numerous titles and banners ascribed to God and to the Lamb.

The inspiration of these words will lead you right into God's presence. One of the ways to pray these hymns is to imagine that your voice is your instrument, and that these words are your notes. Imagine that each of the worship words or victory chants makes a different note, even when they are shouted, not sung. For example, the word *power* would sound different than *wealth*. *Wisdom* would make a different sound than *strength*. And *honor, glory* and *praise*, is distinct from *blessing, thanks*, and *dominion*. Then, lift up your voice like a trumpet (Isa. 58:1; Rev. 1:10), and send your own worship to the courts of heaven. In this way, as we shout the words to him, it is as though we are playing a worship song, spiritually speaking. And, every time we do it, each word sounds beautiful in his ears. This is what the angels do. These words are heaven's response to the raw revelation of God.

As we worship in this way, these staccato-like shouts will also provoke those in the corporate gathering with us. We will incite others to join us, as we ourselves join with the hosts of heaven. Think of it – the angels, the martyrs, the end-time harvest, the one hundred and forty-four thousand, the great multitude in heaven, the twenty four elders, the living creatures, and the entire heavenly host – are all worshipping God along with us! Remember that no one in heaven is quiet. So when you pray the Hymns of the Revelation *out loud* and *loud*, you will be praying on earth just as they do in heaven! It's the next best thing to being there.

LOOK . . . HE IS COMING

John, To the seven churches in the province of Asia:
Grace and peace to you
from Him who is,
and who was,
and who is to come,
and from the seven spirits before His throne,
and from Jesus Christ,
who is the faithful witness,
the firstborn from the dead,
and the ruler of the kings of the earth.

To Him who loves us and has freed us
from our sins by His blood,
and has made us to be a kingdom and priests
to serve His God and Father—
to Him be glory
and power
for ever and ever!
Amen.

Look, He is coming with the clouds,
and every eye will see Him,
even those who pierced Him;
and all the peoples of the earth will mourn
because of Him.
So shall it be!
Amen.

Revelation 1:4-7

THE OVERCOMER'S PRAYER

These are the words of Him
who holds the seven stars in His right hand
and walks among the seven golden lampstands:

He who has an ear,
let him hear . . . what the Spirit says to the churches.

To Him who overcomes, I will give the right
to eat from the tree of life, which is in the paradise of God.

These are the words of Him who is the
First and the Last, who died and came to life again.

He who has an ear,
let him hear . . . what the Spirit says to the churches.

He who overcomes
will not be hurt at all by the second death.

These are the words of Him
who has the sharp, double-edged sword.

He who has an ear,
let him hear . . . what the Spirit says to the churches.

To him who overcomes,
I will give some of the hidden manna.
I will also give him a white stone with a new name written on
it, known only to him who receives it.

These are the words of the Son of God,
whose eyes are like blazing fire
and whose feet are like burnished bronze.

*He who has an ear,
let him hear . . . what the Spirit says to the churches.*

**To him who overcomes
and does My will to the end,
I will give authority over the nations—**
*`He will rule them with an iron scepter;
he will dash them to pieces like pottery'—*
**just as I have received authority from My Father.
I will also give him the morning star.**

These are the words of Him
who holds the seven spirits of God
and the seven stars.

*He who has an ear,
let him hear . . . what the Spirit says to the churches.*

**He who overcomes will, like them,
be dressed in white.
I will never blot out his name from the book of life,
but will acknowledge his name before My Father
and His angels.**

These are the words of Him who is holy and true,
who holds the key of David.
What He opens no one can shut,
and what He shuts no one can open.

He who has an ear,
let him hear . . . what the Spirit says to the churches.

Him who overcomes
I will make a pillar in the temple of My God.
Never again will he leave it.
I will write on him the name of My God
and the name of the city of My God,
the new Jerusalem,
which is coming down out of heaven from My God;
and I will also write on him My new name.

These are the words of the Amen,
the faithful and true witness, the ruler of God's creation.

To him who overcomes,
I will give the right to sit with Me on My throne,
just as I overcame
and sat down with My Father on His throne.

He who has an ear,
let him hear . . . what the Spirit says to the churches.

Revelation 2:1,7-8,11-12, 17-18, 26--29; 3:1, 5-7, 12-14, 21-22*

HOLY, HOLY, HOLY!

Each of the four living creatures had six wings
and was covered with eyes all around,
even under his wings.
Day and night they never stop saying:
"Holy, holy, holy is the Lord God Almighty,
who was,
and is,
and is to come."

Whenever the living creatures
give glory, honor and thanks
to Him who sits on the throne
and who lives
for ever and ever,
the twenty-four elders fall down
before Him who sits on the throne,
and worship Him who lives for ever and ever.

They lay their crowns before the throne and say:
"You are worthy, our Lord and God,
to receive glory
and honor
and power,
for You created all things,
and by Your will
they were created
and have their being."

Revelation 4:8-11

WORTHY IS THE LAMB

And when the Lion of the tribe of Judah
had taken the scroll
from the right hand of Him who sat on the throne,
the four living creatures and the twenty-four elders
fell down before the Lamb.

Each one had a harp
and they were holding golden bowls full of incense,
which are the prayers of the saints.

And they sang a new song:
"You are worthy to take the scroll and to open its seals,
because You were slain,
and with Your blood You purchased men for God
from every tribe and language and people and nation.

You have made them
to be a kingdom and priests
to serve our God,
and they will reign on the earth."

Then I looked
and heard the voice of many angels,
numbering thousands upon thousands,
and ten thousand times ten thousand.

They encircled the throne and the living creatures and the elders.

In a loud voice they sang:
"Worthy is the Lamb, who was slain,
to receive power
and wealth
and wisdom
and strength
and honor
and glory
and praise!"

Then I heard every creature in heaven
and on earth
and under the earth
and on the sea,
and all that is in them,
singing:
"To Him who sits on the throne and to the Lamb
be praise
and honor
and glory
and power,
for ever and ever!"

The four living creatures said,
"Amen,"
and the elders fell down and worshiped.

Revelation 5:8-14

THE MARTYR'S CRY

When He opened the fifth seal,
I saw under the altar the souls
of those who had been slain
because of the word of God
and the testimony they had maintained.

They called out in a loud voice,
"How long,
Sovereign Lord, holy and true,
until You judge the inhabitants of the earth
and avenge our blood?
How long . . . ?"

Then each of them was given a white robe,
and they were told to wait a little longer,
until the number of their fellow servants and brothers
who were to be killed
as they had been killed was completed.

Revelation 6: 9-11*

PRAISE OF THE END-TIME HARVEST

After this I looked
and there before me was a great multitude
that no one could count,
from every nation, tribe, people and language,
standing before the throne
and in front of the Lamb.

They were wearing white robes
and were holding palm branches in their hands.

And they cried out in a loud voice:
"Salvation belongs to our God,
Who sits on the throne,
and to the Lamb."

All the angels were standing around the throne
and around the elders and the four living creatures.
They fell down on their faces before the throne
and worshiped God, saying:
"Amen!
Praise
 and glory
  and wisdom
   and thanks
    and honor
     and power
      and strength
    be to our God for ever and ever.
   Amen!"

Then one of the elders asked me,
"These in white robes—
who are they . . .
and where did they come from?"

I answered,
"Sir, you know."

And he said,
"These are they
who have come out of the great tribulation;
they have washed their robes
and made them white in the blood of the Lamb."

Therefore,
"they are before the throne of God
and serve Him day and night in His temple;
and He who sits on the throne will spread His tent over them.

Never again will they hunger;
never again will they thirst.
The sun will not beat upon them,
nor any scorching heat.

For the Lamb at the center of the throne
will be their shepherd;
He will lead them to springs of living water.
And God will wipe away every tear from their eyes."

Revelation 7: 9-17

TIME TO REIGN

The seventh angel sounded his trumpet,
and there were loud voices in heaven,
which said:
"The kingdoms of the world
has become the kingdoms
of our Lord and of His Christ,
and He will reign for ever and ever."

And the twenty-four elders,
who were seated on their thrones before God,
fell on their faces and worshiped God, saying:

"We give thanks to You,
Lord God Almighty,
the One who is . . . and who was,
because You have taken Your great power
and have begun to reign.

The nations were angry;
and Your wrath has come.

The time has come for judging the dead,
and for rewarding Your servants the prophets
and Your saints . . . and those who reverence Your name,
both small and great—
and for destroying those who destroy the earth."

Revelation 11: 15-18

OVERCOMING THE DRAGON

Then I heard a loud voice in heaven say:

"Now have come
the salvation
and the power
and the kingdom of our God,
and the authority of his Christ.

For the accuser of our brothers,
who accuses them before our God . . . day and night,
has been hurled down.

They overcame him
by the blood of the Lamb
and by the word of their testimony;
and they did not love their lives so much
as to shrink from death.

Therefore rejoice, you heavens
and you who dwell in them!
But woe to the earth and the sea,
because the devil has gone down to you!
He is filled with fury,
because he knows that his time is short."

Revelation 12:10-12

THE SONG OF MOSES

And I saw what looked like a sea of glass
mingled with fire,
and standing beside the sea,
those who had been victorious
over the beast and his image
and over the number of his name.

They held harps given them by God
and sang the song of Moses the servant of God
and the song of the Lamb:

"Great and marvelous are Your deeds,
Lord God Almighty.
Just and true are Your ways,
King of the ages.

Who will not fear You, O Lord,
and bring glory to Your name?
For You alone are holy.
All nations will come and worship before You,
for Your righteous acts have been revealed."

Revelation 15:2-4

JUST AND TRUE

Then I heard a loud voice from the temple
saying to the seven angels,
"Go, pour out the seven bowls of God's wrath on the earth."

Then I heard the angel in charge of the waters say:

"You are just in these judgments,
You who are and who were,
the Holy One,
because You have so judged

for they have shed the blood
of Your saints and prophets and
You have given them blood to drink.
They deserve it."

And I heard the altar respond:
"Yes, Lord God Almighty,
true and just are Your judgments."

Revelation 16:1, 5-7

THE WEDDING SONG

After this I heard what sounded like the roar
of a great multitude in heaven shouting:
"Hallelujah!
Salvation and glory and power belong to our God,
for true and just are His judgments.
He has condemned the great prostitute
who corrupted the earth by her adulteries.
He has avenged on her the blood of his servants."

And again they shouted:
"Hallelujah! The smoke from her goes up for ever and ever."

The twenty-four elders and the four living creatures
fell down and worshiped God, who was seated on the throne.
And they cried:
"Amen, Hallelujah!"
Then a voice came from the throne, saying:
"Praise our God, all you His servants,
you who fear Him, both small and great!"

Then I heard what sounded like a great multitude-
the roar of rushing waters like loud peals of thunder shouting:
"Hallelujah! For our Lord God Almighty reigns.
Let us rejoice and be glad and give Him glory!
For the wedding of the Lamb has come,
and His bride has made herself ready.
Fine linen, bright and clean, was given her to wear."

Revelation 19: 1-8

COME, LORD JESUS!

Behold, I am coming soon!
My reward is with Me,
and I will give to everyone according to what he has done.
I am the Alpha and the Omega, the First and the Last,
the Beginning and the End.
Blessed are those who wash their robes,
that they may have the right to the tree of life
and may go through the gates into the city.
Outside are the dogs, those who practice magic arts,
the sexually immoral, the murderers, the idolaters
and everyone who loves and practices falsehood.

"I, Jesus, have sent My angel
to give you this testimony for the churches.
I am the Root and the Offspring of David,
and the bright Morning Star."
The Spirit and the Bride say,
"Come!
And let him who hears say,
"Come!"
Whoever is thirsty,
let him come;
and whoever wishes,
let him take the free gift of the water of life.
He who testifies to these things says,
"Yes, I am coming soon."
Amen. Come, Lord Jesus.

Revelation 22:12-17, 20

rayer Chart

HOW TO USE THE ORGANIZATIONAL PRAYER CHART

We have included this chart to help you get in the habit of praying the Bible. There is an important philosophy behind it. We have found that everybody needs structure and that good habits are formed through repetition and consistency. For centuries, the people of God engaged in the regular routine of praying the Bible. When you form the habit, the habit forms you.

Children, in particular, need to be taught to pray. In working with our own children for over three years teaching them to pray, we have discovered that, unless something is in place that children can easily follow, the practice dissipates. A daily chart, which they can fill out and bring to you, will not only help them form a habit, it will put the onus on them to get it done. While it makes the prayer time fun, it also forms a discipline. Younger children will benefit greatly by getting it signed by a parent every day.

We also want to underscore the idea of privilege versus punishment. The intention is not to punish children for not saying their prayers. Yet, it is very biblical to withhold privileges. In our household, the way we have worked it is summed up like this: "Pray today, play tomorrow. No pray . . . No play!" If they forget to pray, they lose a privilege; when they have filled out a chart, we reward them. Children like to be rewarded for their efforts.

The chart is fairly self-explanatory. All you really need to do is photocopy it, insert the dates, check off which section of prayers has been prayed, and write down the specific verses of text. Adults and children alike can use the chart to regain the lost art of daily prayers.

Organizational "Praying

Name: _____

Week of: _____

W E E K

Prayer Categories	MONDAY Today I prayed... ☑ Text	TUESDAY Today I prayed... ☑ Text	WEDNESDAY Today I prayed... ☑ Text
Theophanies	❑	❑	❑
Psalms	❑	❑	❑
Wisdom	❑	❑	❑
Songs	❑	❑	❑
Prophets	❑	❑	❑
Jesus	☑	❑	❑
Apostolic	❑	❑	❑
Hymns	❑	❑	❑
Extra Prayers	❑	❑	❑
Prayed # minutes	min.	min.	min
Today I felt...			

the Bible" Prayer Chart

_____

_____

| D | A | Y | S |

THURSDAY	FRIDAY	SATURDAY	SUNDAY
Today I prayed...	Today I prayed...	Today I prayed...	Today I prayed...
☑ Text	☑ Text	☑ Text	☑ Text
❏	❏	❏	❏
❏	❏	❏	❏
❏	❏	❏	❏
❏	❏	❏	❏
❏	❏	❏	❏
❏	❏	❏	❏
❏	❏	❏	❏
❏	❏	❏	❏
❏	❏	❏	❏
min.	_min._	_min._	_min._

ENDNOTES

INTRODUCTION

1. Rabbi Hayim Halevy Donin, *To Be A Jew* (New York: Basic Books Inc., Publishers, 1972), pp.159-160.

THE THEOPHANIES: SECTION 1

1. Peter R. Carrell. *Jesus And The Angels: "Angeology And The Christology Of The Apocolypse Of John"* (Cambridge: Cambridge University Press, 1997) p. 38.

THE PSALMS: SECTION 2

1. "The Psalms," *The International Standard Bible Encylopaedia,* (Biblesoft, The PC Study Bible, 1996).

THE SONG OF SONGS: SECTION 4

1. Fr. Alberto Colunga, O.P., *The Song of Songs: A Mystical Exposition,* (Rockford, Illinois: Tan Books and Publishers, Inc., 1992), Preface, by Fr. Juan G. Arintero, O.P.

2. G. Lloyd Carr, *The Song of Solomon: Tyndale Old Testament Commentaries,* D.J. Wiseman, ed. (Leicester, England & Downs Grove, Illinois: Intervarsity Press, 1984), pp. 114 - 115. ". . . most Palestinian goats have long wavy black hair." Therefore, this is probably a reference to the beauty of her wavy black hair.

THE PRAYERS OF JESUS: SECTION 6

1. Author unknown, Helen Bacovcin, trans., *The Way of a Pilgrim,* A Classic of Orthodox Spirituality, (New York: Image Books, 1978), pp. 23-24.

THE APOSTOLIC PRAYERS: SECTION 7

1. Mike Bickle, *Web-Site Notes on the Apostolic Prayers,* Unpublished, 1998. See www.fotb.com for more information.

Other Books by Wesley Campbell

Welcoming a Visitation of the Holy Spirit
by Wesley Campbell

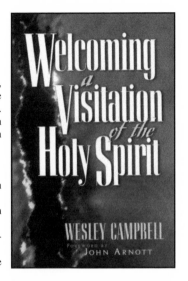

In Welcoming a Visitation of the Holy Spirit, Wesley Campbell takes a refreshing look at the renewal movement known as the Toronto Blessing. He combines the expertise of a biblical scholar with the unabashed enthusiasm of someone who's fallen in love with his Savior all over again.

Learn about:
• Prophecies in 1984 that pointed to events in Toronto in 1994
• Biblical tests you can use to identify a visitation of the Holy Spirit
• The spiritual meanings behind falling down, shaking, and laughing
• New outbreaks of renewal and the future of the movement

The Radical Army
Revival & Social Justice: A Paradigm of End-Time Harvest
by Wesley Campbell & Stephen Court

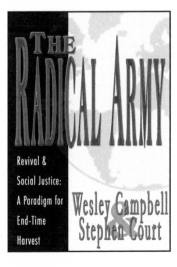

The harvest at the end of the age will come in dramatic sweeps of God's power - revival, and the application of revival to the world as it transforms through social justice.

* Biblical evidence that revivals in Bible transformed the social values of every community.

* A historical look at the success of original radical army - The Salvation Army, and how they transformed England through revival and social justice.

* An up to date look at "children at risk," the plight of the poor everywhere, and how revival is counteracting these global scourges.

PRAYING THE BIBLE SERIES:
OTHER RESOURCES RELATED TO
THE BOOK OF PRAYERS

We would like to offer these additional resources for you to listen to, and use in your own personal prayer and devotional times. These CD's are directly associated with certain genres contained within The Book of Prayers.

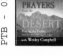

Prayers from the Desert
Praying the Psalms with Wesley Campbell
"Prayers from the Desert" focuses specifically on praying the Psalms in a context of original musical arrangements and accompaniment.
Prayers from the Desert available in CD, Cassette & Instrumental CD

Selah
Singing the Psalms with the Heather Clark Band
After having written the music for "X-treme Disciples" and "The Elijah Revolution" Heather became hooked on Praying the Bible. Taking it a step further she began to sing-pray the Psalms. "Selah: Singing the Psalms was the result. With impacting rhythms and lyrics straight from the word of God "Selah" has become a great favorite with the younger crowd.
Selah - Singing The Psalms available in CD

Psalms & Hymns Vol. 1
Praying with Wesley Campbell
Hebrew Psalms set to all new arrangements of Hymns. Join Wesley Campbell as he prays the word of God as it is written.
Psalms & Hymns Vol. 1 available in CD

Apostolic Prayers
Praying the Apostolic Prayers with Mike Bickle
With revival bursting upon us, this album will inspire you to better pray the revival prayers of the Apostle Paul.
Apostolic Prayers available in CD & Instrumental CD

The Fire of Love
Praying the Song of Songs with Mike Bickle
"Many waters cannot quench love... it burns like a blazing fire, the very flame of the Lord." This prophetic love song is also accompanied by an original musical soundtrack.
Fire Of Love available in CD, Cassette & Instrumental CD

Dark Yet Lovely
Sung by Heather Clark
This CD tells the story of the Song of Songs. These intimate and passionate songs display the love relationship between the Bride and Bridegroom.
Dark Yet Lovely available in CD

The Bride's Anthem
Praying the Adoring Prayers from Revelations with Mike Bickle
Mike Bickle prays the visions of the Apostle John from the perspective of the adoring Bride waiting for her soon coming Bridegroom.
Music by Darryl Taylor The Bride's Anthem available in CD & Instrumental CD

TOLL FREE ORDERING: 1-888-738-4832
resources@revivalnow.com
www.revivalnow.com

OTHER PRAYER CD's IN
THE PRAYING THE BIBLE SERIES:

PTB 05: Prayers for the Harvest
PTB 07: Prayers for X-treme Disciples
PTB 11: Prayers For Israel

PTB 12: Prayers for the Elijah Revolution
PTB 17: Children's Prayer

REVIVAL NOW! WORSHIP CD SERIES:

RNW 02: Fireland: Cry of the Celts
RNW 03: Temple Dance
RNW 05: Cry Mercy

OTHER PRAYER RESOURCES IN
THE PRAYING THE BIBLE SERIES:

These paperback booklets are approximately 75 - 100 pages...

Book #1. Praying the Bible: The Pathway To Spirituality

This mini book is the first in the series that gives an indepth
explanation of the "Praying The Bible" concept.

OTHER BOOKS CURRENTLY IN PROGRESS

Book #2. What are you Praying When you Pray the Bible

This mini book will explore each of the eight particular prayer styles, showing a sample prayer
of each category, and describing how to pray them. This booklet will contain a complete list of
prayers, that belong to each of the seven categories of biblical prayers.

Book #3. Teaching Children to Pray the Bible

This is a book written to parents who want their children to pray. How do they do it? Most parents
do not feel effective in their own prayer life let alone, trying to teach their children how. How do
you teach your children to pray? What does a parent do? This booklet will explain the process
thoroughly, include sample prayers and a weekly check list. The mechanics of how children pray,
and how parents get their children to pray.

Book #4. Praying the Bible through the Ages

Praying the bible is not new. "Praying the Bible Through the Ages" is a fascinating history over-
view of how the greatest saints of all the ages have prayed to God by praying the Holy Scriptures.
This mini-book includes Hebrew Prayer, NT Prayer, The Prayer of the early Church Fathers and
Desert Fathers, Prayer East and West, Eastern Prayer, Benedictine Prayer, Celtic Prayer, The
'Lectio Divina' and Monastic Prayer, Bible Praying of the great revivalists and the modern prayer
movement.

Book #5. Praying The Bible and Revival

This fifth book in the series will explore the relationship between praying the bible and revival.

CONTACT INFORMATION

Bookings for Wesley Campbell:

Revival NOW!
Suite D225A - 2041 Harvey Avenue
Kelowna, BC. Canada
V1Y 6G7
Phone: (250) 717-1003
Fax: (250) 862-2942
E-mail: wesley@revivalnow.com

Conferences & Schools:

Revival NOW! along with New Life Church, host 4 to 6 conferences and 1 to 2 training & equipping schools per year in beautiful Kelowna, BC. If you would like to join us for any or all of these events, please contact us at the above address or check out our website at www.revivalnow.com for more details.

Resources:

Toll Free Ordering: 1-888-738-4832
E-mail: resources@revivalnow.com
www.revivalnow.com